Rats

Complete Care Made Easy

Rats

PRACTICAL, ACCURATE ADVICE FROM THE EXPERT

Debbie Ducommum

BOWTIE
PRESS®

Laguna Hills, California

Nick Clemente, special consultant
Amy Fox, editor
Rachel Rice, indexer
Book design and layout by Michele Lanci-Altomare

The rats in this book are referred to as *he* or *she* in alternating chapters
unless their gender is apparent from the activity discussed.

The Library of Congress has cataloged an earlier printing as follows:

Ducommun, Debbie, 1958-
Rats/Debbie Ducommun
. p. cm.
Includes bibliographical references (p.).
ISBN-10: 1-889540-71-4 (pbk:alk.paper)
ISBN-13: 978-1-889540-71-9 (pbk:alk.paper)
1.Rats as pets. I.Title.
SF459.R3 D835 2001
636.9'352—dc21

              2001001330

BowTie Press®
A Division of BowTie, Inc.
23172 Plaza Pointe Dr., Ste. 230
Laguna Hills, California 92653

Printed and bound in Singapore
15 14 13 12 11 10 09 08   6 7 8 9 10

Acknowledgements

THIS BOOK IS DEDICATED TO MY TEACHERS AND supporters: my mom, who allowed me to fully develop my love of animals; The Rat Fan Club members; and the rats, especially Gremlin, Penny, Cleo, Ranger, Sputnik, Whiskers, Ratster, Gidget, Topsy, Jetta, Kojak, Shoe, Brawny, Prussia, Bandit, Bunny, Slug, Angel, Spot, Arnie, Wylie, Meezie, Gimoo, Bro-man, Tinsel, Shelley, Pixel, Tanya, Dotti, Sissy, Baby, Moses, Teddy, Jasper, Dickens, Harrison, Echo, Lucky, Ernie, Moosh, Smudge, Coco, October, Zelda, Zesta, Harry, Lily, Hexa, and Goblin.

I'd like to acknowledge the special assistance given me by Mary Ann Isaksen, my friend and dedicated rat advocate; and Dr. Barry Dohner, my very special rat veterinarian. They have always been very supportive and willing to share their special knowledge with me over the years. I would also like to thank my husband, Larry, for his wonderful support.

Debbie "The Rat Lady" Ducommun and her chinchilla blaze Berkshire rex rat.

Contents

1

The Remarkable Rat

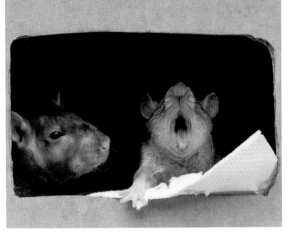

A rat's yawn may be a type of greeting.

You ARRIVE HOME AFTER A BUSY DAY AT WORK OR school. As soon as you walk in the door, little faces with twitching noses eagerly greet you. Tiny pink hands cling to cage wires, and bright little eyes beg to come out. When you open the cage, your rats scramble onto your hands and nestle in your arms so you can rub behind their ears. Then they climb to your shoulder to kiss your cheek and nibble your ear, ready to accompany you wherever you go.

Rats are charming companions who offer love, affection, and nonstop amusement. Many people who get rats for the first time are unprepared for how personable and interactive they are. Every day more people discover what good pets rats are and join the ranks of rat lovers.

A Long Association

The relationship between rats and humans is centuries old. Ancient Egyptians worshipped rats, and in Japan the rat is considered a symbol of wealth. Rice cakes are set out for rats on New Years. If rats gnaw on the cakes, it foretells a good harvest for that year. The Chinese also believe that the rat is a symbol of prosperity. Chinese folklore explain that the rat's intelligence and cunning is the reason it is the first animal of the Chinese zodiac.

Other cultures see rats in a positive light. Hindus especially revere rats because their god Ganesha, the symbol of prosperity, traditionally rides on the backs of rats. There is a rat park in Calcutta, India, where people feed wild rats, and a temple in Deshnoke, India, dedicated to rats. Inside the temple grounds, rats are protected and fed, and they mingle freely with people (wild rats are generally aggressive toward humans only when they are cornered or threatened). Historically, residents of Bassora, Turkey, did not allow rats to be killed, believing they bring good luck.

Although wild rats were probably kept as pets earlier, the first records we have of them being bred in captivity are from the 1800s in England. During this time, a popular sport was "ratting," where dogs were put in pits to kill as many rats as they could. Thousands of

Left: The elephant-headed Hindu god Ganesha is often portrayed on the back of a rat. *Right:* In this temple in India, wild rats are revered and fed by people.

wild rats were captured to supply the pits, and a rat-catcher named Jack Black is thought to have been the first person to breed these rats and sell them as pets.

In 1901, the National Mouse Club in England held the first show where rats were exhibited. The club became the National Mouse and Rat Club in 1912, but after 1918 interest in rats declined, and in 1931 the name *Rat* was dropped from the club. It wasn't until 1976 that the first true rat club, the National Fancy Rat Society, was established in England.

In the first half of the twentieth century, rats were considered suitable pets only for children, although there were certainly adults who enjoyed them as well. One of the best known people who had a pet rat is Beatrix Potter. As a girl, she had an albino rat named Sammy. Rats appeared in many of Potter's stories, and she dedicated one story, first published as *The Roly-Poly Pudding* and later as *The Tale of Samuel Whiskers*, to Sammy. Pet rats have even lived in the White House. Teddy Roosevelt's presidential household included a great many pets, including rats.

In the 1990s, adults began discovering that rats are the perfect pet for a fast-paced lifestyle. Easier to care for than dogs, cats, or birds, rats provide people with the same amount of affection and interaction. As the popularity of companion rats began to grow in the United States, especially in California, membership in rat and rodent clubs began to climb, and pet shops reported selling more and more rats as pets. In some areas of the country, rats have become more popular than hamsters.

Natural History of the Rat

Rats are members of the rodent family. There are more than 1,700 species of rodents, making up over 40 percent of all the world's mammals. Without a doubt, the rat is far more intelligent than most of its relatives. The only rodent possibly smarter than the rat is the squirrel.

Although there are many different rat species, most people think about the two species of wild rats that choose to live near humans. The smaller species of these two rats is the roof rat, *Rattus rattus*, which is also called the black, ship, or tree rat. The roof rat is thought to have originated in India, making its way around the world with human travelers. Its large ears, long tail, and delicate build are better adapted to tropical climates. It was the first species to have reached Europe, with bones found in ancient sites dating back to the third century A.D.

The larger and more common rat is the Norway rat, *Rattus norvegicus*, also known as the brown, common, house, wharf, sewer, and barn rat. The Norway rat is the ancestor of the domestic rat. This rat is thought to have originated in Russia near the Caspian Sea and followed human travelers around the world. The English mistakenly named it the Norway rat because they thought it had arrived on ships from Norway. This rat has small ears, a heavy build, and is suited to cool climates.

The roof rat was the first species to colonize America, with the Norway rat arriving later, in about 1775. In the United States, the roof rat is most common along the coasts, in the South, and in California, while the Norway rat is widespread throughout the rest of the country. In Canada and England, the Norway rat is the dominant species with the roof rat surviving in some ports and islands.

While the roof rat and the Norway rat are closely related, they cannot interbreed. In some areas, the two species can live harmoniously, with the Norway rat occupying sewers, basements, and burrows, and the roof rat living in trees and attics. In many cases, however, the Norway rat, a larger and more aggressive animal, has forced the roof rat to move out. Both species have probably always chosen to live near people where they can benefit from our food and shelter.

Wild rats can do a great deal of damage to human property. They gnaw on buildings, electrical wires, and water pipes, and eat or soil large amounts of food. They can also carry disease. The roof rat was the carrier of the fleas that caused the great plagues of medieval Europe.

Humans have waged war on rats for centuries, first attacking with dogs, ferrets, and cats, and then with traps and poisons. The most effective way to eliminate wild rats, however, is to remove food sources and prevent rats' entry into buildings. One study in Baltimore found that cleaning up the streets and alleys of trash reduced the rat population by 50 to 75 percent.

The wild Norway rat is an adaptable opportunist, able to take advantage of changing conditions. With a tough and athletic compact body, the Norway rat is a good climber, digger, jumper, and swimmer. A slender Norway rat can squeeze her body through any opening big enough for her head, scale a brick wall, leap 4 feet, use utility cables as tightropes, and chew through lead and concrete. The average wild Norway rat weighs only 10 to 17 ounces, although the largest on record was 23 inches long and weighed 2 pounds 12 ounces.

Top right: The adaptable wild Norway rat is the ancestor of the domesticated rat.
Bottom right: The roof rat is the more common wild rat in warm climates and coastal regions.

In cities, wild rats claim small territories: basements, sewers, and walls of buildings. In the country, they live in or under buildings or in fields, and they may range widely looking for food. Their burrows, which can be up to 4 feet deep, can have three to five entrances, an emergency exit, and many rooms. There are rooms for sleeping, food storage, and latrines. Rats line their nesting chambers with soft material and make bigger, more elaborate nests in cold weather.

Rats live in large family groups, or colonies, all sharing the same burrow and defending their territory against strangers. All the rats share in the construction of their burrow. Although they're not true pack rats, Norway rats carry a variety of items to their burrow.

A Rat's Life

Rats are born hairless and blind, totally dependent on their mother. The average litter size for wild rats is eight. The babies, called pups, nurse for about six weeks, although they start eating solid food when their eyes open at fourteen days. Wild rats reach sexual maturity at two to four months of age. When a female comes in heat, the males do not fight over her but take turns mating with her. The gestation period is twenty-one to twenty-three days. Each mother tends to have her own nesting chamber, although more than one rat may share a nest. Babies learn what foods to eat by taking pieces from adults.

Rats are excellent climbers, using their tails to balance and steady themselves as this young patchwork hairless rat demonstrates.

Rats are omnivorous. Wild rats eat plants, seeds, grains, nuts, fruit, insects, worms, eggs, and carrion. Rats are predatory and catch and kill reptiles, amphibians, fish, birds, and small mammals such as mice. Rats search for food both alone and in groups.

Although wild rats eat almost everything, they are wary of unfamiliar foods. A rat nibbles only a little of a strange food at first. If it makes her sick, she avoids that food from then on. Rats also avoid foods with a bitter flavor. Since they are unable to vomit, rats must be careful about what they eat.

The teeth and jaws of a rat, like those of all rodents, are specially designed for gnawing. The four incisors, a pair on the top and on the bottom, are like chisels. They grow constantly throughout a rat's life to replace the worn down enamel. A rat

These hand-raised wild rat pups are just opening their eyes and learning to eat solid food.

also has twelve tiny molars used to chew food. Between the incisors and molars is a space called the diastema where special cheek folds prevent debris from entering the mouth while the rat is gnawing.

Because we see wild rats eating our garbage, they have the reputation of being dirty animals. They really are quite clean though, grooming constantly by licking themselves and then licking their hands to wash their faces. They also use their back toenails as combs.

Rats communicate with each other through scent, sound, touch, and visual signals. Vision is their weakest sense. They are mostly color-blind and nearsighted, although they see movement extremely well and can see in very dim light. Some domestic rats weave their heads from side to side to improve depth perception and to help them focus on stationary objects. Rats who do this may be especially nearsighted.

Rats have excellent hearing and communicate with sounds beyond our range of hearing. Baby rats emit ultrasounds to call their mothers, and males use these ultrasounds when fighting. Rats are silent when playing, but they squeak when annoyed or defensive, and screech when hurt or terrified. They express other strong emotions such as agitation, frustration, or contentment by grinding their teeth.

Body language is important to rats. Rats claim territory or declare their status by shuffling or scraping their hands on the ground. In a confrontation, a rat may hold her tail out stiffly and rattle or vibrate it. An aggressive rat puffs out her hair and arches her back and may hiss. In a fight, rats push their shoulders against each other as a test of strength before grappling and biting. They may also stand on their hind legs and box.

Rats groom themselves constantly and are actually clean animals.

This rat is puffing out his fur and arching his back as a warning.

A rat expresses submission just as a dog does, by putting her ears back, holding her head down, laying down, or rolling on her back. Some rats seem to wag their tails when happy, and some may shudder or shiver when excited or nervous. A rat stretches and yawns when waking up, but this behavior can also be a greeting. A rat who is playful and excited jumps and twists, scampers, and runs around in circles. A curious rat does a lot of sniffing and may rear up on her hind legs. And just like puppies, rats explore new items by licking, nibbling, and chewing on them.

It is unknown how long wild rats live, although studies have shown the average age of colony members is only six months. Wild rats probably do not live past a year or two. As their reflexes slow down, they are more vulnerable to predators such as owls, snakes, foxes, and weasels in the country, and dogs and cats in the city.

Equivalent Aging Schedule

Rat Age	Human Age
5 weeks	10 years
6 months	16 years
9 months	25 years
1 year	35 years
1½ years	50 years
2 years	65 years
3 years	85 years
4 years	100 years
5 years	110 years
6 years	120 years
7 years	130 years

The Domesticated Rat

Domesticated rats are physically much the same as wild rats, and they behave much the same as wild rats, however, the behavior of domesticated rats differs from wild rats in several ways. During the process of domestication, rats were selectively bred to be more docile and accepting of human handling and restraint. Domesticated rats are less aggressive, less fearful of humans and new objects, and less predatory than their wild counterparts.

Domesticated rats reproduce more quickly than wild rats, reaching sexual maturity earlier (as early as five weeks) and having bigger litters. These are the same qualities that separate other predatory domestic animals, such as dogs and cats, from their wild ancestors. Domesticated rats are true domestic animals and would have trouble surviving on their own in the wild.

Young domesticated rats do not need to be tamed—they need to be socialized. Every animal species has a critical period of development when it most easily bonds to other individuals. In rats, the critical socialization period is two to six weeks of age, with two to four weeks being the most critical. Handling and petting baby rats of this age for just a few minutes each day ensures that they are socialized to humans, and the more they are handled, the friendlier they will be.

Fully socialized rats accept people as part of their family, interacting with their two-legged family members as if they, too, were rats. Rats will groom, play, sleep, and eat with the human members of their family. It is this ability to form strong social bonds that makes rats such delightful companions.

These young rats are learning to trust people through socialization.

Varieties of Rats

Rats haven't been domesticated long enough for true breeds to develop, but many varieties of rats exist. Currently, there are thirty colors, ten patterns, six coat types, and three body forms that can be mixed and matched, with new varieties being developed all the time. Most pet shops carry only smooth-coated rats in the most common colors—agouti, black, beige, and white—in either solid or hooded patterns. The hooded pattern is unique to rats; they appear to be wearing a colored hood over the head and shoulders, with a stripe or patch of color down the back.

Rats can be found with rex, velvet, velour, or satin coats, and some have hardly any hair at all. Rex rats have curly hair. The velvet coat is short and plush, while velour is short and fuzzy. A satin coat is extra shiny.

This show rat's coat has agouti coloring with a rex texture.

Patchwork hairless rats have short hairs that grow in, fall out, and grow back in other places. They usually look a little different each week.

Hairless rats can have pink or dark skin. In one type of hairless rat, called the patchwork hairless, short hair grows in patches or stripes that seem to move around as the hair falls out and grows in elsewhere. Other hairless rats retain short sparse hair on their faces all the time, while some are completely hairless except for their whiskers. All hairless and rex rats have curly or crinkled whiskers. One rodent club calls its hairless rats sphynx after a hairless breed of cat.

Although some people are repelled by the naked skin of a hairless rat, many are not and think hairless rats look more like people. Some people admit the hairless is their favorite variety of rat. Hairless rats look and are more vulnerable and require some special care. They can't tolerate extreme cold, although they do fine at temperatures down to 65° Fahrenheit (F). Since they don't have eyelashes, some of them get debris caked under their eyelids, which needs to be cleaned out whenever it accumulates to prevent eye damage. Their delicate skin is also vulnerable to scratches. Some patchwork hairless rats die soon after birth, and some hairless females have trouble producing milk.

Another variety of rat is the odd-eyed. These rats have eyes of different colors, usually one red or pink, and the other black or ruby red. Odd-eyed rats are more common in certain colors, but breeders are trying to develop them in all colors and varieties.

One of the newest varieties of rats is the tailless, or Manx rat. Like Manx cats, Manx rats have a different posture than rats with tails. While these rats are popular with people who feel squeamish about the natural long tail, Manx rats do need some special care. A rat's tail acts as a heat exchanger and helps to regulate body temperature. Without this special organ, a tailless rat is susceptible to heatstroke and should be kept in temperatures

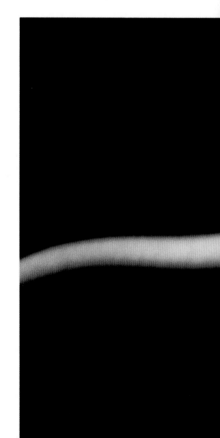

A lynx-colored odd-eyed rat

below 80° F. Some Manx rats can have deformities of the spine or abnormalities of the bowel because of poor breeding.

Another new variety of rat is the Dumbo. These rats have slightly larger, thicker, and more rounded ears that are set low on the sides of their head, giving them a cuddly and sweet appearance.

Each rat, whether she is white, beige, rex, hairless, or Manx, will exhibit the same basic rat behavior, modified by her own personality, of course. A rat's personality does not depend on her appearance. Any rat, as long as she receives human socialization when young, makes an excellent and loving companion.

2

Are Rats the Right Companions for You?

Many rat lovers never want to be without rats again.

Rats are intelligent.

Rats have many characteristics that make them especially suited to being companion animals. Like other pocket pets, rats are small, clean, quiet, and easy to care for, but rats are much more intelligent than hamsters, mice, gerbils, guinea pigs, or rabbits. Pet rats easily learn their names and come when called. They can even learn to perform tricks.

Extremely social animals, rats enjoy interacting with people. This combination of intelligence and sociability means rats form close personal bonds with people, show us affection, and enjoy being petted. They love to have their heads rubbed and many lick their owners as a sign of affection. They also need regular interaction with other rats, so it's a good idea to get at least two rats.

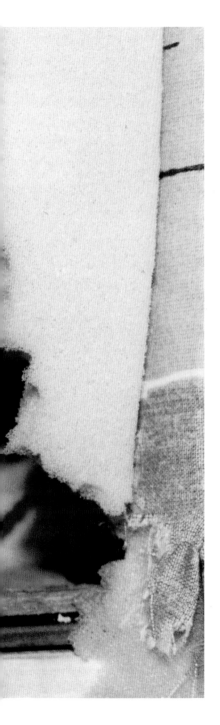

Rats are playful and can play games with people. They're smart enough to learn how to wrestle with your hand and play other interactive games such as peekaboo, tag, tug-of-war, and hide-and-seek. Rats can be just as playful, affectionate, and interactive as dogs, but rats don't bark and don't have to be taken for walks!

Naturally nocturnal, rats are awake and ready to play in the morning and evening when most people are home from work or school. If the house is empty during the day, they're content to sleep, but rats can easily adjust their schedules to match those of their human companions.

Most rats have a tendency to chew. If your rat is a chewer, you may want to keep him away from your valuables and furniture.

Because rats groom themselves constantly, they have almost no odor. They don't need you to groom them or brush their teeth. Keeping their cages clean and providing fresh food and water is about the only work rats require, but they do need a lot of attention and playtime because they're so social. They must have the opportunity to spend time outside their cages on a regular basis to play, explore, and interact with you. If you want a pet just to watch, you'd be better off getting hamsters, fish, or some mice.

There are a few rat characteristics that some people find objectional. Some rats chew on things. This behavior is usually worse when rats are young, but just like puppies, rats often grow out of the tendency to chew. Although some rats never seem to chew on things, you must expect that most rats occasionally chew on wood, paper, plastic, and fabric.

Some people develop a skin rash after handling rats. This is usually a contact irritation, not a true allergy; wearing clothing and washing after handling your rats prevents most problems. Rex and hairless rats cause fewer problems for some people. Some people get itchy skin welts from rat toenails that are so sharp they penetrate the skin without the person noticing. Skin lotion containing aloe vera soothes scratches. True respiratory allergies to rats are not common, but if allergies run in your family, it's recommended you keep rats out of the bedroom.

Health problems, especially respiratory infections and tumors, are common in rats, and it is often difficult to find a veterinarian experienced in treating rats. It's recommended that rat owners educate themselves and get involved in the treatment process to ensure their rats receive proper health care.

The one rat characteristic that disappoints most people is the rat's short life span. The average life span of a healthy rat is two to two and a half years, but some rats can live three years or even up to five years. In some situations, this short life span can be an advantage. You don't need to make a commitment of ten to twenty years to a rat like you do to a dog or cat, but most people want their animal companions to live as long as possible. By giving your rats the best health care, nutrition, exercise, and love, you can help extend their life span. It is painful to lose a friend after only three years, but those of us who love rats believe the enjoyment outweighs the pain.

If you want a pet who's friendly and loving, playful and curious, intelligent and active, quiet, small, and easy to care for, then a rat is what you're looking for!

More Than One Rat

Because rats are social animals, they should live with other rat friends.

It isn't healthy for a rat to live alone. Rats groom each other and play and sleep together. No amount of human attention can replace the company of another rat. Two or more rats keep each other company when you can't play (such as in the middle of the night) and provide security for each other. Single rats often seem to be more easily stressed and can be more prone to disease. Some single rats even develop behavioral problems or neurotic tendencies. If you choose to have just one rat, you must interact with him for several hours every day. Otherwise the poor rat will be living in a state similar to that of solitary confinement. Caring for two rats doesn't take much more work than caring for one. As long as each rat receives individual attention from you, each will bond to you.

Roommates should be of the same sex, unless you have one or both neutered, because a fertile male and female may produce a litter of up to sixteen babies every four weeks! Since rats normally live in family groups, same sex pairs can get along equally well if they grow up together or are properly introduced. Some good-natured squabbling is all you should expect to see among rats with an established relationship.

The Cost of Keeping Rats

Rats are inexpensive to care for. Rat blocks (large pellets of food formulated specifically for rats) generally cost $1 to $2 per pound; the annual expenditure for food for two rats is about $24 to $60 per year. The costs for litter and bedding depend on which types you use, and whether you use a litter box or cover the bottom of the cage with litter. Generally the cost ranges between $40 and $100 per year for two rats.

The most significant investments for pet rats are the initial costs for the cage and accessories, and the cost of having your rats spayed or neutered. Commercial cages can cost $60 to $100 and up, while homemade cages cost much less. Cage accessories cost another $10 to $20. The cost of the rats themselves generally ranges from $3 to $5 for the common varieties and up to $20 for more exotic types. Unfortunately, the low initial cost for most rats has encouraged many people to consider rats to be disposable pets. This attitude, however, is changing as people recognize that a price cannot be put on the individual personality of a rat.

Top left: Rats groom each other and play, eat, and sleep together. If you have only one rat, you will need to spend a lot of time with him.
Bottom left: Rats live in groups in the wild, so it is natural for domesticated rats to need and enjoy the company of other rats.

More and more people recognize that rats deserve proper care, including veterinary care, regardless of a rat's initial cost.

Aside from the costs of spaying or neutering, veterinary costs for a rat can vary widely. A rat with active mycoplasmosis (a contagious and incurable, respiratory infection) will need periodic treatment. The costs for this depend on whether over-

the-counter treatments are sufficient or if veterinary care is necessary. As with other animals, older rats are more likely to need veterinary treatment than younger rats. You should count on spending between $50 and $200 a year on veterinary care for a rat. Veterinary Pet Insurance offers major medical health insurance for rats, which may help with costs.

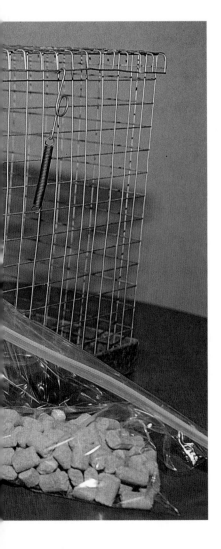

Your rats will need a variety of items such as a cage and cage accessories.

MYCOPLASMOSIS

MYCOPLASMOSIS IS THE MOST COMMON HEALTH PROBLEM SEEN IN RATS. The microorganism Mycoplasma pulmonis causes a respiratory infection. A rat can be infected without showing symptoms, but mycoplasmosis eventually causes respiratory disease in most infected rats. Mycoplasmosis can also cause lung damage even if there haven't been any overt symptoms.

Mycoplasmosis can be carried by guinea pigs and is contagious and incurable in rats and mice. The severity of a mycoplasma infection is increased by cigarette smoke, ammonia from a dirty cage, genetic susceptibility, vitamin A or E deficiency, and a concurrent respiratory infection of another type.

The first symptom of mycoplasmosis is sneezing. The sneezing might go away and then come back again. Even if you don't hear sneezing, you may see the results: red spatters on the walls or bedding. The red color comes from a pigment in rat tears that run down into the nose and are sneezed out. After several months, the symptoms usually progress to wheezing. People sometimes mistake wheezing for the rat "talking," but any noise made while breathing is wheezing. Wheezing can sound like grunting, squeaking, chirping, or "monkey sounds." Eventually, the lungs are damaged and the rat exhibits labored breathing. The symptoms may then advance to acute respiratory distress, which causes rats to gasp through their mouths or dash about in panic when they can't get enough air. If treatment cannot prevent this distress, then euthanasia is the kindest action.

A rat with mycoplasmosis is usually active and eats normally throughout the progression of the disease. Treatment with antibiotics is necessary when wheezing or other severe symptoms occur. Different strains of mycoplasmosis are susceptible to different antibiotics, so your vet may have to recommend several. Secondary bacterial infections can occur along with the mycoplasma infection and can result in an acute infection that has a more rapid onset of symptoms, including lethargy, loss of appetite, runny eyes and nose, and labored breathing.

Time Requirements

Compared to many other pets, rats require a minimum amount of care. It takes five to fifteen minutes a day to feed rats, including the preparation. Cleaning the cage takes fifteen to thirty minutes a week. Every month or so, you'll probably want to do a more thorough cleaning, which might take an hour.

In the beginning, you should devote about fifteen minutes a day to teaching a rat to come when called. Once this goal is reached, you won't need to spend any more time training your rats unless you want to. Teaching your rats various games and tricks, however, not only increases the bond between you and your pets, it also helps to develop their brains and personalities.

You can include your rat in many of your everyday activities.

The only other time requirement your rats need is the time you spend playing with them. It's important for your rats to get out of their cage at least five times a week, but every day would be even better. Rats are happiest spending at least two hours a day out of their cages. While you don't need to interact with your rats during this whole time, it's best if you are available to supervise and interact with them as they desire. You can let your rats run around while you watch TV, write letters, or do homework, as long as you can occasionally stop what you're doing to pet or play with them. The more you interact with your rats, the more intelligent, enjoyable, and happy they will be.

Vacations

Rats present few problems when planning a vacation. Rats travel well, so one option is to take them with you! You might get a small cage just for trips. It's best to get rats used to traveling while they are still young. When getting your rats used to traveling for the first time, try to keep them in a quiet environment, and don't let strangers handle them until they have adjusted to the change.

Once rats are used to traveling, you don't have to care for them any differently than you do at home, but there are a few things to remember. Remove the water from the cage while on the move to prevent dripping. When you stop for breaks, offer water to your rats and give them a chance to drink. Never leave your rats alone in the car when the temperature is warm. Rats are sensitive to heat and easily die from heatstroke. If you have a wire cage, you must protect it from the sun with cardboard, an umbrella, or cloth (rats may pull it into the cage and chew on it).

If you plan to travel with your rats, it's a good idea to keep a smaller cage around to use as a travel cage.

When traveling in warm weather, bring water and ice to cool your rats if necessary.

If you can't take your rats with you, there are several options depending on the amount of time you'll be gone, but leave your rats home only if the temperature of your house can be controlled. If you're planning to be gone for three days or less you can leave your rats with enough food and water to tide them over. If your rats are free roaming or live in an open-type condo, you should confine them to a closed cage to prevent problems while you're gone.

If you'll be gone longer than three days, you might know a friend who will rat-sit for you. If your house is temperature controlled, a friend or neighbor would need to visit your home only once a day to replace the food and water, keep the cage clean, and visit with your rats to make sure they are all right. But it might be more convenient for someone to take your rats to his or her home.

A friend who has rats would probably be the best choice for a rat-sitter. You could take turns caring for each other's rats. If your rats are free from mycoplasmosis, make sure your friend's rats are too before letting her or him take your rats home. You should decide beforehand if you will allow your friend's rats to play with yours. Unless the rats already know each other or are young, it's not a good idea to let them interact.

If you don't know anyone who will rat-sit for free, you could hire a pet-sitter to visit your home, or there may be a nearby veterinary hospital or kennel that boards small pets. No matter who cares for your rats, make arrangements well in advance and write out any special instructions, especially about where to put the cage if your rat-sitter is taking it. Also, be sure to leave this book with them for reference.

Rats and the Law

Rats are legal as pets in most places around the world. Pet rats are not allowed in Billings, Montana, or in Alberta, Canada. Laws and ordinances can change, so you should always check with your local lawmakers to be sure it's legal to keep rats as pets in your area.

Just because it's legal to keep rats, however, doesn't mean that all landlords and public entities greet them with open arms. Some landlords refuse to allow rats in their buildings. People who keep several cages of pet rats are sometimes seen by social workers, police officers, and even humane society staff as being eccentric or even crazy. These attitudes are all a holdover from the aversion to wild rats. The only way to combat negative attitudes toward rats is to confront them. Most people are not aware of the positive characteristics of rats, and many are curious and accepting once these are explained to them. While there are always people who have a strong fear of rats, or who absolutely refuse to consider them in a positive light, general attitudes are changing. The more we talk about our rats to others, the more rats become accepted as animal companions.

3

Choosing a Rat

This exceptionally trusting adult rat was well socialized as a baby.

So YOU'VE DECIDED TO GET RATS! BEFORE LOOKING FOR your new pets, it's a good idea to decide whether you want them for companions only or if you might want to show or breed them. While you always want to choose healthy, personable, attractive rats, potential show rats or breeding stock should be particularly good examples of their variety.

Sources for Rats

Most people think of getting rats at a pet shop, but there are four other sources you should consider: animal shelters, occasional breeders, hobby breeders, and laboratories.

A pet shop may not be the best source for rats. Unfortunately, many shops treat rats as nothing more than food for snakes and aren't concerned with their health or temperament. Some pet shops buy their rats from large breeders who are also unconcerned. Ask where the shop's rats come from.

The best pet shops separate their male and female rats. Domesticated rats reach sexual maturity very early—as early as five weeks of age. If you buy a female older than this from a mixed group, she'll most likely be pregnant.

While unwanted rats aren't as common as homeless cats or dogs, some animal shelters get a large number of rats who need homes. A shelter might also offer discounts on spaying or neutering.

Another source is someone whose companion rat has had an unplanned litter of babies. You can find out about these rats by newspaper ads, on community bulletin boards, on Web site adoption pages, or by word of mouth. Ask around at local schools. In this case you can check out the mother's health before picking out any of the babies.

A hobby breeder is likely to be an excellent choice for a healthy, well-bred baby rat. A good breeder selects breeding stock based on personality, appearance, health, and longevity, so ask what the breeder's goals are. If he or she has no goals, the health and quality of the animals may not be high. A good breeder is knowledgeable about mycoplasmosis and tries to selectively breed rats who show a natural resistance to the disease.

A breeder may not have babies for sale at all times, but it's worth waiting a few weeks for a quality animal. A hobby breeder is the best source for some of the more unusual varieties of rats. To find out if there's a hobby breeder in your area, ask at your local pet shops or contact a rat club near you.

If you're buying your rats at a pet shop, look for a shop that sells rats as pets and separates males from females.

Some laboratories, especially those at universities, give away surplus rats who would otherwise be destroyed. The laboratory rat is the same animal as the pet rat, except more inbred and specialized. Laboratory rats are free from mycoplasmosis—an advantage over rats from other sources, although the choice of colors is limited, and laboratory rats aren't usually as well socialized as those raised for pets. If you get a baby, though, extra socialization is all it takes to make a fine, healthy companion. Older lab rats sometimes make good pets, but it depends on how much socialization they've received. A rat who willingly approaches your hand to sniff or nibble your fingers will likely make a suitable companion.

One of the newest and most popular rat colors is blue.

What to Look For

The most important characteristics to look for when choosing a rat are good health and personality—in that order. A healthy rat is active, curious, and has bright, shiny eyes; she sniffs the air and swivels her ears in response to sound. When held, both babies and adults should feel solid, not fat or bony. Avoid a rat who looks bloated. A sick rat is often hunched up, lethargic, and unresponsive. Although fear can cause a rat to freeze, in time she usually relaxes. Fear can also cause diarrhea.

Be sure to check rats for symptoms of respiratory disease, the most common health problem. The most common symptoms of mycoplasmosis are sneezing and wheezing. Wheezing is more noticeable after exercise, so try to get a rat in question to run around, then hold her up with her chest to your ear to listen for wheezing. It's also a good idea to make sure that any rat you consider buying is checked by a veterinarian.

Both male and female rats make good pets, but they tend to have different characteristics as adults. A female is smaller than a male and generally is more active throughout her life. Some females hardly slow down long enough to be petted. Males are usually more sedentary, making better lap pets, and they can get quite fat as they age if they don't have adequate exercise. Males are more likely to mark their territory with urine, but many females also urine-mark. The urine usually doesn't stain, but the behavior can be annoying. If this behavior bothers you, you might want to get males and have them neutered since neutering usually stops the behavior in males. There is no way to stop urine-marking in females.

Sexing young rats is easy once you know how to do it. Don't rely on the word of a pet shop employee; examine the rats yourself. The sex differences are most clear when you hold a male and female side by side, so compare rats until you find two who look different. In a male, the anus and genitals are separated by the scrotum, while in the female they're much closer together.

In general, outgoing rats make the best companions, but choose one whose personality appeals to you. A properly socialized rat won't hesitate to sniff or nibble on your fingers.

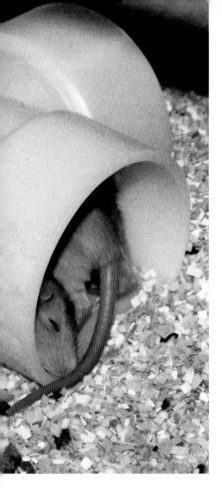

When choosing a rat from a group, you may want to let one of the rats choose you. That way, the bond between you and your rat may be especially strong.

It's best to choose a rat four to six weeks old, which is when a rat is most socially adaptable. If your choices are limited and you have to choose between a shy four-week-old baby and a four-month-old adolescent who begs to climb your arm so she can nibble your ear, don't hesitate to pick the older rat. Any rat who is that friendly, regardless of age, makes an excellent companion.

Instead of picking out the rats yourself, you might want to let the rats pick you! Put your hand down in the cage to see if any of the rats have a special interest in you. Making the choice a mutual decision is the best way to start a great friendship.

4

Your Rats' Home at Home

Rats seem to love sleeping and playing in cardboard boxes.

Before getting your rats, you must decide how you will house them. Both wire cages and those with solid sides such as aquariums have advantages and disadvantages. You should choose the type of cage you mind cleaning the least. You can also create a combination cage by stacking a wire cage on top of an aquarium or joining one or more wire cages and/or aquariums with tubing. For two rats, a cage should be at least 14 inches x 24 inches wide and at least 12 inches high. A larger cage is even better. It's a good idea to have an additional smaller cage as a travel cage that can also be used to isolate new or sick rats.

Wire cages provide the best ventilation. Since wire mesh floors can severely irritate a rat's feet and cause infection, solid floors are preferred. If your cage has a wire floor, cover it with a material such as plastic needlepoint canvas. This material is flexible, easy to cut, easy to clean, and it protects a rat's feet from the wire while allowing liquids to run through.

Cages made of 1-inch x ½-inch mesh are dangerous to rats because a back foot can get caught in the mesh, causing a wrenched or even broken leg. A cage for baby rats should be made of ½-inch square mesh or bars ½ inch apart or less. A cage for adult rats can be made of bars, 1-inch square mesh, or 1-inch x 2-inch wire. You could get a small cage suitable for babies at first, and as they grow, get a larger one. The small cage can then be used as a travel cage.

The bottom pan of a wire cage should be at least 2 inches tall to prevent litter from being kicked out. A nice feature is a tray that can be pulled out without disturbing the rest of the cage, but look at the design carefully. Many cages have edges around the tray that collect debris, requiring more extensive cleaning. Rat urine corrodes metal, so try to find wire cages protected by a coating. It's even better if the pan is made of plastic.

Aquariums need to be cleaned more often than wire cages because they lack ventilation. The larger the aquarium, the better the ventilation; 20-gallon size is minimum, and larger is better. In hot weather, it's a good idea to run a small fan across the top of the aquarium to improve the ventilation.

Aquariums are cleaned easily with a small dust pan and broom to scoop out old litter, or you can suck the dirty litter out with a wet/dry vacuum. Then it's easy for you to wipe the bottom and sides clean. Some rats chew on the silicon sealant around the edges of aquariums, but it doesn't seem to hurt them.

Weekly cage cleaning keeps the chore manageable and your rats healthy.

You can buy a screen top for an aquarium, or you can make your own out of ½-inch square mesh. If you don't have a dog, cat, or ferret in the house, you may not need to cover the aquarium. As long as the aquarium is up on a stand, dresser, or shelf, most rats won't jump out of it (they *will*, however, climb down a wire cage). A rat may occasionally fall to the floor, so never leave your rats unattended for more than a day if they live in an open cage.

If you have the space, a homemade giant rat condo makes an excellent home for rats.

This same principle holds for the open-style condo, which might be a table, or a collection of shelves and/or open cages for your rat's home. The surface of the table or shelves should be covered with a nonporous material such as glass, vinyl, or Formica to allow for easy cleaning and to discourage chewing. Wood surfaces absorb urine and become smelly unless they are protected with a waterproof finish. A child's plastic wading pool up on a table makes an especially good rat condo. A condo can also be used as a playground.

Once rats are used to the freedom of an open-style home, they may become frustrated if confined to a closed cage. Since there may come a time when you need to confine your rats to a closed cage, it's best to get them used to one first before giving them more freedom. Also, an open-style playground or home won't work for all rats. Some are much too adventurous and learn how to jump or climb out to go exploring.

The best location for the cage is in a room where your family gathers in the evening. Rats love to interact with people and are happiest in a room where activity takes place. Some owners even report that their rats seem to enjoy watching TV!

A cage should be placed on a table, dresser, or stand to avoid drafts and cold spots on the floor. Never place the cage near a window because of drafts and because the heat of direct sunlight can quickly kill a rat. Place the cage away from a heater or air conditioner.

Rats need a period of complete darkness at night. If they are constantly exposed to light they can be more prone to tumors. Female rats can develop fatal cystic ovaries. Avoid night lights in the room, and cover the windows.

A Rat's Basic Needs

Cage: *At least 14 inches x 24 inches wide and 12 inches high. Wire cages provide much better ventilation than aquariums. For adults, cages can be made of 1-inch square mesh or 1-inch x 2-inch wire. Rats can get their legs caught in mesh that is 1 inch x ½ inch.*

Companionship: *Rats are social and are happiest in pairs or groups. Choose rats of the same sex, or alter your rats. Single rats are not recommended as pets.*

Food: *The basic diet should be rat blocks. Supplement with fresh foods such as fruits, broccoli, kale, bok choy, tomato, cooked beans, and sweet potato.*

Food Dish: *Buy a food dish that is heavy enough so it can't be tipped. Hanging FoodHoppers also work well.*

Nest Box: *Rats like a cozy place to sleep. A variety of clean household items such as milk jugs, cans, jars, and ink-free boxes can be used and are easily replaced when needed.*

Safe Litter and Bedding: *Rats need clean litter and bedding. Do not use cedar or pine shavings; they contain toxic hydrocarbons. Instead use aspen shavings or the many safe commercially prepared litters on the market.*

Water Bottle: *Keeps the water clean. A hard plastic wide-mouth bottle is best.*

Litter, Bedding, and Furnishings

Litter is material placed in the bottom of the cage or litter box to absorb urine, while bedding is material used to make a nest. Unfortunately, the most common products used for litter are pine shavings or cedar chips because they are inexpensive and smell good. But both pine and cedar are toxic to rats. The same oils that give the chips their pleasant odor are toxic, and these aromatic hydrocarbons are inhaled and absorbed into a rat's body where they must be eliminated by the liver. The long-term effect of this can be liver disease, a depressed immune system, and retarded reproduction. Acids in the shavings damage the respiratory tract and can increase respiratory infections. There is even evidence these woods can cause cancer. The toxic oils in pine wood are the active ingredients in Pine-sol, a brand of disinfectant that kills germs.

Although aspen shavings are safe to use, there are many safe commercially prepared litters on the market that are more effective at controlling odor and less messy to use than wood shavings. Some of these are made from recycled paper or commercial by-products such as aspen bark or grain chaff. Alfalfa pellets or rabbit food also make good litters for rats. Corn cob litter, made from ground corn cobs, can be used with caution as some rats try to eat it and get it caught in their throats. Do not use clay or sand cat litters. New brands of litters are appearing all the time. To evaluate them, investigate the ingredients and be sure to avoid any containing pine or cedar.

In cold weather, rats like to curl up in bedding. Some rats wet their bedding, so check it often and change it when necessary. Shredded paper makes good bedding, but avoid using paper with ink on it. Petroleum-based inks are toxic, colored inks usually contain toxic lead, and even nontoxic soy ink rubs off on a rat's fur and skin, requiring additional grooming. It is safe to use nonprinted newspaper (purchased from your local newspaper), the perforated edges that are torn off continuous-feed computer paper, white paper towels, or white facial tissue.

Many people like to use rags, cotton, or yarn for bedding, but these materials should not be used for a maternity nest or with young rats. Baby rats can get legs or heads tangled in loose threads. Felt, on the other hand, is perfectly safe and makes particularly warm bedding. A commercial shredded corn husk bedding is also a good choice. Hay, both grass and alfalfa, can be used as long as it's not dusty or moldy.

There is a wide selection of safe cage litters available. Try several types until you find one you like.

Safe Litters and Bedding

LITTERS

Healthy Pet Milled Grain (Absorption Corporation) 800-242-2287: These pellets of grain by-products have a nice smell and control odors quite well.

Critter Country (Mountain Meadow Pet Products, Inc.) 800-752-8864: The company claims these pellets made from wheat grass actually prevent the formation of ammonia.

Aspen Supreme Pellets (Green Pet Products, Inc.) 800-405-6378: These pellets have the advantages of aspen shavings without as much of the mess.

Yesterday's News (Nestle Purina Petcare) 800-778-7462: These pellets are made from recycled newspaper with an odor absorbing ingredient. The brand comes in regular pellets and softer texture pellets.

BEDDINGS AND LITTERS

CareFRESH (Absorption Corporation) 800-242-2287: This product is made from wood pulp fibers too short to make paper. The fibers are processed to the appearance and texture of shredded egg cartons, and they can be used as both litter and bedding.

Eco-Bedding (Fibercore) 800-658-6150: Thin, crinkled strips of kraft paper (brown paper, one grade below grocery bags) make up this bedding, which is recyclable even with animal waste. It makes a better bedding than litter.

It's a good idea to train your rats to use a litter box if you're going to let them roam freely.

Always keep fresh, clean water available in a chew-proof container that prevents spilling.

In warm weather, bedding isn't necessary, but rats still like to sleep in a nest box. Plastic containers work well since they can be washed, and many rats like oatmeal boxes. Be sure to use only ink-free boxes or remove the printed label. Cardboard boxes, soft plastics such as milk jugs, and fabrics will probably be chewed. This doesn't seem to hurt rats, but the items have to be replaced periodically. Cardboard items need to be replaced if wet or dirty. Some rats like jars or cans, especially when it's hot. Rats like their beds to be up off the floor, so consider hanging the nest box in the cage. This saves floor space, too.

A water bottle helps keep your rats' water clean. The best water bottles have a mouth wide enough to accommodate a bottle brush for cleaning. Since some rats chew on soft plastic water bottles, hard plastic or glass bottles are best. Before filling the water bottle, let the water from the tap run until cold to reduce the amount of toxic lead that leaches into the water from pipes and faucets. If your tap water is chlorinated, it is best to use bottled or filtered water.

Rats sometimes like to move their food dishes around and pile litter over them to hide their food, so either a heavy dish that can't be tipped, or one that attaches to the side of the cage is best. Lixit makes special hanging food dispensers called FoodHoppers that are highly recommended. Provide two food dishes or dispensers—one for dry food and one for moist food—and be sure to wash the container used for moist food daily.

Food for Your Rats

A nutritious low-fat, low-calorie diet will help keep your rats healthy. Studies have shown that some legumes, fruits, and vegetables help prevent cancer. Soybeans are especially known for this. The easiest diet to feed rats is rat blocks, large pellets formulated especially for rats. Rats have different nutritional requirements than other animals. The best rat blocks contain a large proportion of soymeal, rather than corn. Rat blocks should be available to your rats all the time. You may choose to feed your rats a homemade rat diet such as the one offered in the appendix. Do not attempt to make your own diet.

A mix of seeds and grains is a highly popular diet for rodents, but many rats pick out and eat only their favorite bits. This not only causes waste but also may result in an imbalanced

You may choose to feed your rats a combination of a mixed grain diet, nutritious rat blocks, and fresh fruits and vegetables.

diet. Many of these mixes contain a large amount of rabbit pellets, which are mostly indigestible for rats. If you do choose to feed a mixed grain diet, use only a commercially packaged brand fortified with all the nutrients rats need. Generic grain mixes sold in bulk do not provide an adequate diet for rats. Store the blocks or grain mix in an airtight container to help preserve the nutrients.

Fresh foods are an important part of a rat's diet because they contain cancer-preventing compounds, enzymes, and other beneficial components that can be destroyed during processing. If you feed your rats commercial rat blocks or rat mix as a basic diet, the blocks or mix should make up 80 percent of the diet, with vegetables, fruits, and other fresh foods making up the other 20 percent. These fresh foods are the only treats you should give your rats. Commercial small animal treats such as yogurt drops tend to be high in fat and sugar.

Rats like such a variety of healthy foods, you don't need to give them junk food. To prevent obesity, feed high-fat treats such as nuts to your rats only occasionally. Fruit is the healthy way to satisfy a sweet tooth. Table scraps are okay, but keep in mind your rat's small size and give only tiny bits.

Free Run of the House

Many people ask if it's possible to let their rats have free run of the house. Yes, it is possible, as long as you accept that they might do some damage. Before giving your rats free run of the house, you should train them to come when called. Supervision is recommended, but some people let their rats run loose all the time. Giving rats the freedom to roam the house allows them to develop their personalities and use their intelligence to the fullest.

Even if rats have free run of the house, they should still have a cage with food dishes, water bottle, nest box, and possibly a litter box they can retreat to whenever they wish. You may want to confine your rats to their cage on occasion, such as when you have guests.

The two biggest problems you must deal with in a free-roaming situation are chewing and soiling. Most free-roaming rats do a certain amount of chewing on baseboards, wallpaper, furniture, bedding, and carpet—although some rats chew less than others. Younger rats tend to chew more, so many people don't let their rats have free run of the house until they're older. To minimize the damage, rat proof the house and provide plenty of chew toys. If you allow your rats access to only a couple of rooms, they might chew at a door or door frame to get out to where people are. As for soiling, some rats will return to their

You might find your rats in the least likely places if you don't rat proof the rooms they play in.

cage to eliminate if they have the choice. Most rats will also use a small litter box placed in a corner of the room. Sometimes rats choose a different corner than you have in mind, and it's easier to follow their wishes than change their habits.

Urine-marking is a problem. Males should be neutered before being given the freedom of the house. Since females and neutered males can urine-mark, you might want to protect upholstered furniture with washable throw covers. Carpeting and upholstery will probably need to be shampooed on a regular basis.

Rat Proofing

The first step to rat proofing a room is to seal up any holes in the walls, floor, or under cabinets, and make sure all heater vent covers are secure. Examine the underside of the couches and beds and repair torn material.

Rats have been known to chew on any items left out. Move any valuable furniture or other items you don't want chewed to a rat-free room. Chewing of baseboards and other wood surfaces can be deterred with products made to prevent chewing (available at pet stores) or a product that prevents

Close up holes in walls and furniture, and look before sitting when your rats are roaming about in the house.

fingernail chewing in people. Metal guards will provide more permanent protection. Remove access to electrical wires either by fastening them out of reach up along the walls or protecting them with a conduit. You might want to switch from an electric clock to a battery or windup clock, or just remove electrical items from the room.

If your rats have access to the bathroom, keep the toilet lid closed. Rats have been known to fall in the toilet and drown. Do not let your rats walk across cages containing unfriendly rats. The rats inside the cage may bite the interlopers' toes.

Make it a family rule that when rats are loose on the floor, humans in the house do not wear shoes. Rats have a tendency to get underfoot and can be badly injured if accidentally stepped on or kicked by a shoe-clad foot. Stepping on a rat's tail with a shoe is likely to tear off some skin or even break bones. Stepping on a tail barefoot or with a soft-soled slipper causes less injury.

Medications, cleaners, or any other poisonous substances must be stored out of reach. Rats are curious and often chew into containers hoping they contain food. Just because a medicine or cleaner may taste or smell unappealing to you doesn't mean your rats won't find it tasty. Keep cigarettes, ashtrays, and candy away from your rats, too. Don't smoke around rats because the smoke aggravates their respiratory infections, and don't let them run around where you've applied pesticides.

Rats love to burrow under piles of clothing and blankets, so be particularly careful if your rats are around while you're doing laundry. You don't want to add your rats to the washer or dryer! Upholstered furniture can also be dangerous to rats. If your rats are small enough to crawl behind the cushions or, even worse, down behind the box springs, they could suffocate when someone either sits down or gets up. You should always know where your rats are before anyone sits on or gets up from upholstered furniture. Recliners are especially dangerous.

If one of your rats is missing, be sure to look everywhere, even places you wouldn't suspect. Check all closets, cabinets, drawers, containers, and even trash cans. A good way to find a missing rat is to call his name and then listen carefully.

Sometimes you can hear him scratching or rustling. Don't move around immediately after calling your rat. Give him some time to respond before moving on to the next location.

Rats enjoy snuggling in fabric, so check the washer and dryer loads carefully before tossing them in or starting up the appliances.

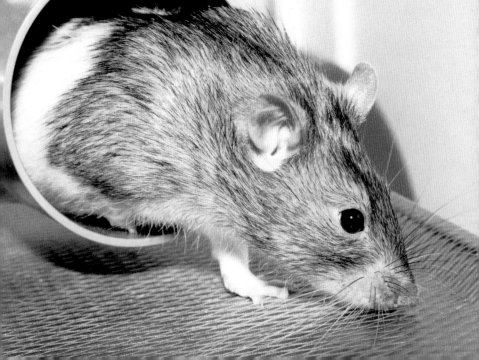

Toys for Your Rats

Rats enjoy climbing on, under, or through tubes, ladders, branches, ropes, and hammocks. Inspect rat toys carefully for dangerous parts. Especially look for sharp edges, small holes, or slits where a rat could get his toes caught.

Tubes can be made from plastic sewer pipe, soda bottles, tennis ball containers, cardboard tubes, and hollow logs. They should be large enough for your rats to easily scamper through. Tubes can even be hung from the side or top of a cage. One combination rats really enjoy is a cloth sleeve attached to the end of a tube. The tube allows rats to enter and exit the sleeve easily.

You can make a playhouse for your rats by taping small cardboard boxes together next to or on top of each other. Cut doors in the boxes so your rats can go from box to box. Paper bags are fun, too, especially when stuffed with shredded, ink-free paper.

Thick ropes and branches encourage your rats to climb and can be used to provide access to the upper levels of the cage. You might be able to get branches from your local tree trimmer. Avoid branches from evergreen or walnut trees, which are toxic. Wash branches thoroughly with soap and water before putting them in the cage. You may also have to wash branches and ropes as part of your cage cleaning regime or replace them when needed. A cinder block placed either upright or on its side makes a good climbing toy and helps to wear down sharp toenails.

Top left: If you have a two-level cage, ladders are a good way for rats to get from one level to another, plus ladders can be great fun!
Bottom left: This agouti hooded rat enjoys exploring a tube.

In general, toys sold for hamsters, hamster exercise balls in particular, are too small for rats. Many toys sold for birds or ferrets, however, work well for rats. Even some children's toys, such as plastic doll houses, make interesting toys for rats to climb in and on. Some rats enjoy Ping-Pong balls.

One of the best toys for inside the cage is an exercise wheel. Some rats become wheel fanatics, and most rats use a wheel to some extent, especially if they learn to use it while young. A rat wheel must be at least 10 inches in diameter, and the best wheels are made of solid metal or plastic, not wire. When buying a metal wheel, make sure there is space between the uprights and spokes of the wheel to minimize the chance of your rat's tail getting caught between them.

Food toys, toys that make your rats work to get a treat, help keep rats occupied. The Ferret Roller Basket from Super Pet is a 2½-inch plastic mesh ball that twists apart so you can put treats inside (flake cereals work best). Pieces fall out as your rat rolls the ball along the floor. There are also several food toys designed for birds that also are fun for rats. The Jungle Talk Carousel treat dispenser works best with fruits and vegetables. The rats must reach through the bars of the carousel to get the treats.

Homemade food toys are easy to make. A cardboard toilet paper tube can be a sort of rat piñata. Place a treat inside and fold the ends over to close it. You can also simply fold a treat inside a crumpled piece of paper so your rats have to unfold it to get the treat. Another fun food toy is the treasure chest. Layer a small box or container such as a shoe box or cookie tin with shredded paper or straw and sprinkle with a few treats. Your rats will have fun digging through the box to find the treats.

Many children's toys, such as this doll's chair, are enjoyed by rats, but keep in mind that the toys will be chewed by most rats.

Allowing your rats to dig for treasures
exercises their burrowing instincts.

Because rats are burrowing animals, many of them enjoy digging in dirt. Given the opportunity, some rats dig up potted plants. To avoid this problem, give your rats their own digging box. Plastic storage containers 12 to 16 inches tall work well. Fill the box halfway with potting soil and keep it moist. Your rats will need a ladder, branch, or cinder block to get into the container. If your rats tend to use their digging box for a litter box, periodically remove the top layer of soil and replace it.

To acquaint your rats with the joys of digging, bury some treats in the soil, or toss a handful of grain and seed mix into the box. You can even plant some wheat grass or other edible plants in the box for your rats' nibbling pleasure. If your rats throw dirt out of the container, you can put it inside a large cardboard box or wading pool to contain the mess.

5

Beginning Your Friendship

Spend some time getting to know your rat
before you pick her up.

BEFORE BRINGING HOME NEW RATS, BE SURE THE
house has been rat proofed and the cage is set up with food,
water, and a nest box. Place the rats in their new home to let
them explore and become familiar with it.

When they seem comfortable, perhaps after an hour or
so, invite them one at a time to come out on your hand. If your
rats have been socialized, they will eagerly climb into your
hand and nestle in your arm or on your shoulder. A rat who
isn't well socialized, or one who is timid, may not accept your
attention. She may try to run away from your hand, squeak
when you try to pick her up, or jump out of your hand. In this
case, spend extra time socializing your rat and teaching her to
trust you.

This socialization process should include frequent gentle handling of your rat. Start by petting her in the cage and then inviting her on your hand. In most cases, this gentle petting and handling helps convince your rat that you are trustworthy. Another good way to build trust with your rat is to teach her to take treats from your hand. You can use a spoonful of baby food to lead her out of her cage and onto your hand.

If a new rat doesn't take food from you at first, it doesn't necessarily mean she doesn't trust you. It may be the food that she mistrusts. Rats are naturally suspicious of unfamiliar foods, especially if they've only eaten one type of food while growing up.

To get rats to trust a new type of food, place a bit of the food in your rats' cage, so they can taste it at their leisure.

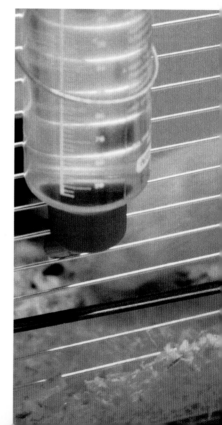

It takes time to build healthy relationships. Consistency and patience will pay off in the long run.

Eventually, your rats will take the food from your fingers. Whenever you hand feed your rats, give them a signal such as saying the word *treat*. This way your rats will know when you have food and when you don't, and they won't try to grab your finger thinking it's food.

Some rats tend to be grabby with food, while others take food gently. If you have a rat who is the grabby type, hold the food so it sticks out past your fingers, or place the food either in the palm of your hand or on a spoon. Rats who mistakenly grab a finger instead of food usually notice this quickly and release the finger. Sometimes a rat is so excited by the food, she accidentally punctures a finger with her sharp teeth. Most people bitten by pet rats receive their wound in this manner.

Help build your rat's trust in you by using two hands to pick her up.

When you first begin handling a new rat, chances are the rat will relieve herself on you. With experience, most rats learn to control themselves. You can encourage this learning process by returning your rat to her cage (or by setting her on a paper towel) frequently. For babies or new rats, these "potty breaks" should come about every fifteen minutes. Older rats can usually last thirty to sixty minutes between breaks. Also, let your rat relieve herself after waking, before taking her out. Although your rat can learn to control herself, she still might urine-mark you. You might want to keep a towel or tissue handy for wiping up the small drops of urine your rat may leave on your skin.

To pick up a rat, use two hands to gently scoop her up from underneath. This method will make her feel most secure and trusting. In some situations, you may need to pick up a rat with only one hand. In this case, grasp her around the chest. Then as you lift her, bring your other hand underneath to support her feet. Rats don't like their feet to dangle.

Instead of picking up your rat, try holding your hand out flat in front of her to see if she climbs aboard. If your rat trusts you, she will learn to climb on your hand because she knows she gets to come out of her cage.

Once a rat is in your hands, bring her close to your body. Rats feel most secure when they have something solid to press up against. You can pet the rat in this position. Rats enjoy being stroked just as cats and dogs do, and rats especially love being rubbed gently on top of the head, behind the ears, or on the cheeks or shoulders. Each rat has her own favorite spot.

A rat hates being picked up by her tail. The only time you should do this is if you need to break up a fight between two rats—and then hold the tail only by the base. The end of a rat's tail is fragile and the skin can actually come off. If you have to lift your rat by her tail, get support under her feet as soon as possible.

When you're ready to put the rat back in her cage, either lift her off your hand and place her gently in the cage or allow her to walk off your hand on her own. However, your rats may enjoy being with you so much they won't want to get off your hand!

Once your rats feel comfortable being held in your hand, they'll probably start exploring and climbing around on your arm. They may even climb your arm to your shoulder—a convenient place for rats to perch. If you have long hair, your rat probably will like crawling under it and cuddling against it.

When you have a rat out with you, it's a good idea to wear older clothing. Most rats just can't seem to resist nibbling on fabric, and there is no way to train them not to. Rats have sharp claws, so wear a shirt that covers your shoulders and neck to protect your skin against scratches.

Understanding Mutual Grooming

Rats maintain social bonds and express affection by grooming each other. They lick each other and nibble off flakes of dry skin. Rats take mutual grooming very seriously. You may observe one rat holding down another while grooming her. It's almost as if the rat is saying, "Now hold still and let me show you how much I love you!"

When we pet rats, they think we are grooming them. Rats most commonly groom each other when they're in a quiet or sleepy mood, so if your rat doesn't want to be petted, it's probably because she's wide awake and wants to be active. Some rats enjoy being petted for only a short time. This is

Many rats, such as this beige hooded rat, like to perch on shoulders.

because grooming can be a sign of dominance and dominant animals don't like to submit to lengthy grooming sessions unless they're in the right mood.

If you have a shy rat, she may prefer to be under a cloth or inside a box when you pet her. This makes her feel more secure. You'll know if your rat wants to be petted because she holds her head down, waiting for you to rub it. She may express enjoyment by grinding her teeth or even bulging her eyes in and out. She may close her eyes, lie down, and even go to sleep! Some very trusting rats even lie on their backs. When rats have had enough petting, they move away from you.

Once a rat has bonded with you, she may begin grooming you in return, most often by licking. The rat may also nibble groom you. This might startle you at first, but it usually doesn't hurt. If it does hurt, you should squeak and pull away. This is how another rat would react, and it teaches your rat to nibble more gently. Not all rats nibble groom people. Anyone who is nibble groomed by a rat should feel honored because it means the rat has bonded to that person so completely that she treats him or her just like another rat.

Sometimes rats groom themselves and other rats excessively. A rat who obsessively grooms herself or another rat, causing bald spots, is said to be exhibiting barbering behavior. The most common area for self-barbering is the front legs, and the most common areas for barbering another rat are the head, face, neck, and shoulders. Because this behavior doesn't usually cause health problems, there is no reason to separate a barber from her roommates, unless you are showing your rats.

Rats groom one another to bond and express affection for each other.

Your rats may even affectionately groom you!

Cleaning

Rats are naturally clean, but they won't stay that way if their cages are allowed to get dirty and smelly. How often a cage needs to be cleaned depends on its size, type, the number of residents, the type of litter, and the temperature and humidity. It helps to scoop out soiled litter in between major cage cleanings.

If the cage smells bad, you're not cleaning it often enough. Cages get smelly because urine is broken down by bacteria into ammonia. Ammonia is very caustic and highly irritating to the respiratory system. Prolonged exposure to ammonia can actually damage the respiratory tract. Set up a schedule and clean the cage before it gets smelly.

Use only a thin layer of litter (about ¼ inch) in the litter box or on the bottom of the cage. A thick layer of litter is wasteful because it has to be changed just as often. It should take only fifteen to thirty minutes to change and clean a cage. If it takes longer, you're probably either letting it go too long, using too much litter, or you have a badly designed cage.

When you change the litter, wipe out the cage with water and a liquid antibacterial soap to help kill germs. Wire cages tend to accumulate grime and need to be scrubbed periodically with a brush. You should also wash the food dishes and water bottle when cleaning the cage. Disinfectant isn't necessary for routine cleaning, since using soap and water removes most bacteria.

Rats and Children

Once they have been shown the proper way to handle their little friends, most children over the age of eight can be trusted to interact with rats safely without adult supervision. Most children under the age of eight and rats can get along with adult supervision. Don't expect any child to take full responsibility for a rat's care. For the well-being of any pet, an adult should be responsible for all care, with the child sharing some tasks.

It's not a good idea to let a rat climb on young children or let children under the age of six hold rats in their arms. Unless the child's clothing is quite thick, a rat's sharp toenails can penetrate the child's delicate skin and cause discomfort. The child might react by dumping or throwing the rat to the floor.

The best way to allow a young child to interact with a rat is to have the youngster sit on the floor and place the rat in his or her lap. You may want to put a folded towel on the child's lap for protection. You can encourage the rat to stay by putting her in a basket. A basket also allows the child to carry the rat in relative safety and comfort. A child can also carry a rat in the front pouch of a sweatshirt.

Scooping out dirty litter in between major cleanings keeps odors at bay.

Male rats, being more content to sit in a lap than females, make the best companions for younger children. Rats older than one and a half years are also more content to stay in one place.

For rats who prefer to explore rather than be petted, the best way to interact with children is through a game. A child may enjoy building a maze out of wooden blocks for the rats, pulling a string for the rats to chase, or hiding treats so the rats can hunt

Rules for Preventing Rat Bites

RATS RARELY BITE, BUT JUST LIKE DOGS OR CATS, RATS CAN BITE UNDER certain circumstances. They defend themselves and their territories (cages) if they feel threatened and may bite in self-defense if scared, startled, or in pain. Rats are wary of strangers and may bite if an unfamiliar person reaches into the cage or pokes a finger through the wire or in front of the rat's face. If their family includes pups, rats can be especially defensive.

Rats may also bite if they mistake your finger for a piece of food or something equally exciting. If you feed your rats through the wire of their cage, they may get into the habit of grabbing anything that's poked in, even fingers.

Here are some rules to help prevent you from getting bitten by pet rats:

- Wash food odor off your hands before playing with your rats.

- Never tease your rats, especially with food, and don't feed them through the wire of the cage.

- Give your rats a consistent signal when you give them treats so they won't get in the habit of always grabbing your fingers.

for treasures. Some rats are happy to explore the house while sitting in a small box a child can pull around the floor like a wagon. If the rat doesn't enjoy this activity, she will jump out of the box.

The keys to successful play between young children and rats are proper adult supervision and understanding the abilities and limits of the child. There is much more danger of the child hurting the rat than the other way around.

- *Instruct visitors and children not to stick their fingers through the wires of the cage, and always take your rats out of their cage before letting strangers pet them.*

- *Use care when there are baby rats in the cage. It's best to take a mother rat out of the cage before examining or playing with her babies.*

- *Be very cautious when handling rats who are scared, aggressive, or hurt. It's a good idea to wrap them in a towel before picking them up.*

- *Be cautious with a new rat, especially an adult. Until she gets to know you, she may not trust you and may bite if you reach inside the cage for her. Try inviting her out of the cage first.*

- *Don't startle a rat by grabbing at her too quickly. Talk to her first, making sure she's awake and that she knows you're going to pick her up.*

- *Handle your rats frequently. Rats who are not handled for a long period of time may become distrustful or neurotic and start biting.*

Introducing Rats

Introducing a new rat to established resident rats should always be done gradually. Never just plop a new rat in a cage because the residents always defend their territory. The willingness of a rat to accept a new roommate depends on the rat's personality, age, and experience. It generally takes more time to introduce a newcomer to adult rats than to baby rats. Do not try to introduce a rat under six weeks old to an adult male because there is a tendency for males to kill babies.

The introduction process has several steps. You can advance to each successive step as long as there is no sign of aggression after thirty minutes.

Before you introduce the rats, quarantine the new rat for at least two weeks (you can use your travel cage for the newcomer). The quarantine area should be as far from your resident rat as possible (a friend's house is recommended), and you should carefully wash your hands and change your clothing after handling the new rat. This is because respiratory infections can be transmitted both through the air and on hands and clothing. If the new rat develops symptoms of illness such as sneezing or wheezing, consult a veterinarian and wait until the symptoms clear up before making introductions.

After the quarantine period, place the cages near each other so the rats can see and smell each other, but keep them far enough apart so the rats can't reach through the bars to the other cage; otherwise, the rats may end up with bitten toes and tails.

Next, switch the rats to each other's cage. This allows them firsthand experience with each other's scent. You may have to do this several times.

A bathtub makes a good neutral place to introduce rats because neither rat feels the urge to defend territory.

Introduce the rats in neutral territory—someplace the resident rat is not used to. This gives the rats a chance to become acquainted without the resident feeling the need to defend her territory. The bathtub is a good place, but remember to cover the drain if you don't have a grate or screen over it already.

After the rats have a chance to meet, give them some treats. Eating together helps them bond. Don't leave them together unsupervised. Move them to an area where the resident is used to playing, and let them interact there. Watch them carefully because fighting may break out. A rat expresses aggression by puffing up her fur, arching her back, and swinging her body sideways at the newcomer. If this happens, remove the newcomer quickly to prevent an attack.

Thoroughly clean the resident rat's cage to remove odors, and rearrange the furnishings so it appears to be new. Before placing them in the cage together, clip their back toenails to minimize scratching in a scuffle. Dab the rats with vanilla extract or perfume to make them smell alike, then put them in the cage together. The best time to introduce them is in the morning when rats tend to be sleepy. The resident will probably sniff the newcomer and then pounce on her, forcing her over on her back. Don't rush to take the new rat out.

Observe whether the resident rat is showing the signs of aggression. If so, remove the newcomer, but if not, leave them together. The resident rat must establish her dominance, and it's normal for her to beat up the newcomer. Just because the new rat is squeaking doesn't mean she's getting hurt. This is just a rat's way of saying, *I give up*. As long as the new rat isn't being injured, you should let the altercation run its course.

The resident rat will probably beat up the newcomer frequently for the first few days, but in most cases the scuffle will be over quickly. The first attack is usually the worst, and before long the two rats typically become the best of friends, sleeping together and grooming each other.

Because each rat is an individual with her own personality, occasionally two rats take a dislike to each other. In this case they constantly fight, sometimes to the point of inflicting wounds. Neutering any males involved usually solves the problem. Otherwise, such rats should be separated.

Introducing Rats to Other Animals

Rats and other animals can sometimes get along, but it depends on the individual pets' personalities. The introduction must be done cautiously. Most problems result from predatory instincts. Dogs, cats, and ferrets are all predatory animals. Rats are also predatory and sometimes attack and kill smaller animals, especially birds. Predatory attacks from rats can occur without warning, so it's not a good idea to introduce a rat to a smaller animal.

Rats sometimes get along with animals, such as rabbits and guinea pigs, but rats have been known to bully such animals, so care should be taken. Keeping different species in the same cage is not recommended. Each species should have its own home, and the two should interact only under human supervision.

When introducing a rat to a predatory animal, such as a dog, the rat is most at risk. During the first introduction, one person holds the rat, and another person either holds the dog or controls her with a leash. Speak calmly to the dog, mildly warning her to be nice. Let the dog and rat sniff each other. It's a good sign if the dog licks the rat, but watch carefully for signs that the dog may be thinking about eating the rat such as the dog licking her lips or attempting to nip the rat. If either the rat or the dog attempts to nip the other, you should say *no* and shake the offender by the scruff of the neck (very gently for the rat).

The next step is to have the dog lie down on the floor and allow the rat to approach on her own. The dog should still be under human control. Another person must be ready to scoop up

the rat quickly if the dog gets out of control. Again, calmly tell the dog to be nice. You want the dog to stay calm and in place. If the dog gets too excited, pick up the rat and remove the dog from the room. You want to teach the dog that she cannot inter-act with the rat unless she stays calm.

If the dog appears to be aggressive toward the rat, avoid further encounters. It's not worth the risk. Certain dogs such as terriers, dachshunds, huskies, malamutes, chow chows, and Akitas are particularly prone to predatory behavior toward small animals. Some large dogs such as malamutes have been known to rip cages apart to kill the rat inside, but any dog potentially can be aggressive toward rats.

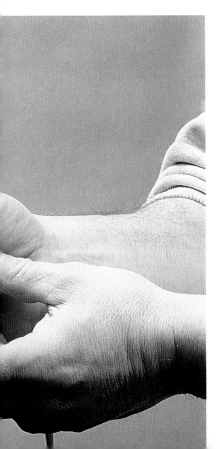

Use care when introducing rats to larger animals such as cats and dogs.

Some rats may act aggressively toward dogs or cats. In this case, it's best if the dog or cat is confined to another room when the rat is out, although it's possible to retrain the rat using systematic desensitization. This involves rewarding the rat for good behavior as you gradually bring the dog or cat closer. Consult an animal trainer for help.

Some rats can get along with other animals if they are introduced carefully. But no matter how well your rat seems to get along with your other animals, it's safest to let them interact only under adult human supervision. It doesn't take much rough play to accidentally injure a little rat.

Teaching Rats the Rules of the House

To teach your rats, you need to communicate with them, and communication is a two-way street. You can teach your rats better if you learn to read their body language so you'll know their likes and dislikes. For example, a rat who doesn't want what you're offering will often push it away with her hand. If you're holding a rat and she wants to go somewhere, she will point and bob her head in that direction. A rat who is tired of an activity will turn or move away.

The first thing you should teach your rat is her name. You may want to wait a few days after getting a new rat before naming her to make sure you pick a name that fits her personality. A rat can learn her name quickly if you always say it when greeting her, inviting her to come out of her cage, and giving her a treat.

Next, teach your rats to come when called. Hold a treat a few inches from one of your rats so she has to come to get it. Say

Rats can become the best of friends with other species.

her name and the words, *come get treat.* Gradually make her come farther and farther to get the treat. Practice this exercise so your rat learns it well.

Many rats have a natural tendency to use a litter box because it's instinctive for them to relieve themselves in one place. The best way to assure that your rats use a litter box is to make sure the box is easy to get to. Some rats are lazy and won't make the extra effort to get to an inconvenient box. In a two-story cage, you may need a litter box on each floor. Outside the cage, the litter box should be near where your rats spend most of their time. More than one litter box might be required, and rats usually prefer that a litter box be placed in a corner.

You can use treats to teach your rat to come.

If your rats learn to use a litter box in the cage first, they might be more likely to use a litter box outside their cage. The secret to training your rats to use a litter box in the cage is to inspect the cage frequently. Clean up any urine, but pick up any droppings you find in the cage and move them to the litter box. Eventually, your rats will get the idea that the litter box is the designated latrine.

If you are observant, you will learn to recognize the characteristic posture of a rat getting ready to relieve herself. If you see one of your rats assume this posture outside the litter box, gently pick her up and place her in the litter box.

Catching a Frightened Rat

Most rats escape from their cages not to run away but to explore. When they're finished exploring, they just might climb into bed with you! But what if a frightened, nonsocialized rat finds her way out of her cage? Or what if your rat, frightened about being loose, finds a cozy hiding place and refuses to come out?

The most likely places for a rat to hide are under a refrigerator, couch, or bed. It's even possible for a rat to climb inside a couch or box spring if the lining underneath is torn, so don't let anyone sit on a couch until you find your rat. Look carefully under the refrigerator because some have a type of shelf underneath where your rat can climb up off the floor.

If you have dogs or cats in the house, it's wise to put them either outside or in a room you're sure is rat free. If your dog is good friends with your rat, however, he might be able to help you find her.

The best way to lure your rat out of hiding is with her favorite soft treat on a spoon. If necessary, you can cover her

with a towel before picking her up. Another way to lure your rat out of her hiding place is to put a treat inside your rat's nest box and set it down where she can get to it. This may tempt your rat to get inside the familiar, safe box to eat, allowing you to pick her up—box and all. You can also place your rat's cage near her hiding place to tempt her to return to it.

If all else fails, you can buy or rent a live trap from an animal shelter or feed store. Use a live mousetrap for baby rats and a squirrel trap for adults. Bait the trap with your rat's favorite treat, or try a smear of peanut butter on the trigger. The sooner you find and catch your rat, the better. The longer frightened rats stay loose, the harder they are to catch.

Rats may hide if they become frightened.

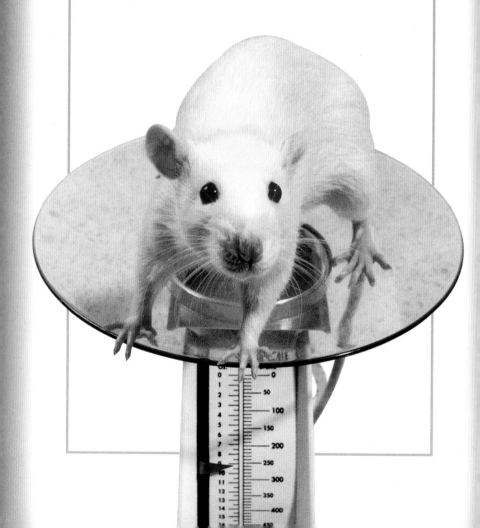

6

Rat Health Care

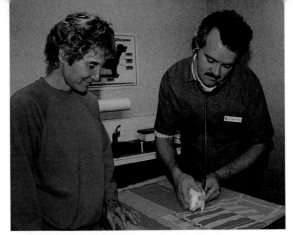

Find a veterinarian who is knowledgeable about rats.

Choosing a Veterinarian

WHILE YOU CAN EXPECT MOST VETERINARIANS TO BE knowledgeable about cats and dogs, most vets don't know much about rats. Veterinarians do not receive adequate training in the treatment of rats at veterinary schools. Instead, they must gain knowledge about rats through seminars and personal experience.

Some vets, with the best of intentions, believe they can treat rats without any special knowledge. They may not realize that rats have special needs regarding surgical and nursing care. Therefore, to be a responsible rat owner, you must educate yourself and get involved in the treatment process to make sure your pet receives proper care.

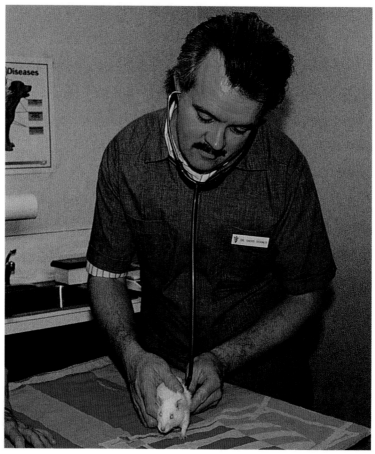

A good veterinarian will fully examine your rat and ask you a lot of questions about his medical history.

If you can't find a veterinarian who is experienced at treating rats, try to find one who likes and respects them and is open and willing to learn more about them. Unfortunately, there are some veterinarians who have no respect for rats—those vets should be avoided. If any veterinary staff members make a derogatory comment about rats, be sure to tell them you don't appreciate such an attitude.

How to Locate a Qualified Rat Vet

The Rat Fan Club and the Rat and Mouse Club of America maintain referral lists of qualified veterinarians. If they do not list a veterinarian near you, call all the vet offices in your area, and ask if they treat rats or to whom they refer their rat patients. Generally one or more vets in an area establish a reputation as the "exotic" animal vet.

If you find a vet who treats rats, ask the receptionist to have the doctor call you when it's convenient. When the vet calls, ask how he or she feels about rats as pets (of course, the vet should like and respect rats) and how many rats he or she treats each year (hopefully more than just a few). Ask what type of rat surgeries the vet has performed (removing tumors, neutering, and spaying should all be included) and the success rate (which should not be less than 95 percent). Ask the vet how familiar he or she is with mycoplasmosis (he or she should be very familiar with the symptoms and treatment) and if he or she requires an overnight fast for rats before surgery (the answer should be no). The answers to these questions will give you an idea of how knowledgeable and experienced a vet is in treating rats. It's important that you feel comfortable with your veterinarian, so choose one who is easy to talk to. If the veterinarian seems informed and has a good attitude toward rats, the next step is to take one of your rats in for a basic exam.

What if the local exotic vet doesn't pass muster? Then you must try to find another vet who is willing to learn more about rats. Although this process can be time consuming and expensive, it's the best way to ensure that your veterinarian is a true working partner with you in the health care of your rats.

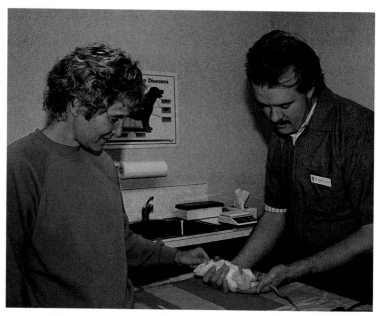

It's important to be involved in your rat's medical treatment.

Then—and this is very important—if your rat needs medical treatment, read up on the problem yourself so you can be involved in the treating process. Don't be afraid to question your vet about a particular treatment. After all, you know your rat best! Only through this type of action and encouragement will the proper treatment of rats become commonplace among veterinarians.

First Visit to the Veterinarian

The best way to transport a rat to the veterinary hospital is in a small carrying cage. Provide a nest box for him to hide in, or cover the cage with a cloth. If you don't have a carrying cage, use a small cardboard box. Bring a small towel to cover the cold metal exam table in case the vet doesn't provide one. Get your rat out of the carrying cage yourself, and set him on the towel.

A qualified veterinarian will examine your rat's eyes, mouth, ears, and all body parts. The doctor should palpate (feel up inside) the abdomen and listen to the heart and lungs with a stethoscope. She or he should handle your rat gently but firmly without fear or nervousness. The veterinarian will take your rat's history, asking you about his age, diet, type of cage, bedding, litter, and previous health problems. Mention any concerns you might have, treatments you've read about, and ask the vet for recommendations.

The Benefits of Spaying and Neutering

Spaying and neutering small animals is becoming more common. There are both behavioral and health benefits to having these surgeries done.

Spaying drastically reduces the incidence of mammary and pituitary tumors, both of which are quite common in female rats. Mammary tumors are usually benign and can be removed surgically, but many unspayed rats develop multiple tumors requiring several surgeries. Pituitary tumors, which are always fatal, can cause a variety of neurological symptoms, including loss of coordination, impaired use of the legs, and lethargy. Up to 70 percent of unspayed female rats develop either mammary or pituitary tumors in their lifetime, while only 4 percent of spayed rats develop these tumors.

Both these tumors are caused by hormonal changes that occur in female rats when they stop ovulating (usually around eighteen months of age). Spaying removes the ovaries, which are the source of the tumor-causing hormone. Spaying also eliminates the chance of cancer or infection of the ovaries, uterus, and cervix. This can be especially important for rats who are infected with mycoplasma, since this disease can cause abscesses and bleeding of the uterus. Spaying and neutering prevent unwanted litters and allow males and females to live together. Because of these benefits, spayed rats tend to live 25 percent longer than unspayed rats.

The best time to have a rat spayed is when she is between three and six months of age, but it can be done at any age. Spaying a rat is similar to spaying a cat and costs about the same (and is usually less expensive than having a mammary tumor removed). It's best if the female is spayed when not in heat.

Neutering male rats (best done at three to four months of age) also has its benefits. Intact male rats usually do quite a bit of urine-marking, and their backs can get oily, causing a greasy appearance and feel. Some males also develop an overabundance of testosterone, which leads to aggression toward other rats and even people. Neutering males solves these problems, since the hormone-producing testicles are surgically removed. Neutering also eliminates the chance of cancer or infection of the testicles, reduces the incidence of kidney degeneration, and may decrease the chance of prostate disease.

Although it is commonly thought that spaying and neutering animals makes them fat and lazy, this just isn't true. A survey done about dogs actually found that neutered dogs were more active than intact dogs. If your rat gets fat, it's because he's eating too much and not getting enough exercise!

Typical Health Problems

Rats are susceptible to many of the same diseases that afflict humans and other animals as well as those diseases specific to rats.

It is common for un-spayed female rats to get multiple mammary tumors.

Keep alert for any changes in your rats' behavior or appearance. If you notice unusual symptoms in one of your rats, take him to your vet as soon as possible. Lethargy, in particular, is a serious and urgent condition in a rat. Be prepared for an unexpected, after-hours emergency by asking your vet for referrals to emergency clinics before an emergency takes place. In an emergency, be sure to call the hospital first to let them know you're coming so they can be prepared to help as soon as you arrive.

Respiratory disease is the overriding health problem and cause of death in rats. Mycoplasmosis and two viruses, the Sendai virus and Sialodacryoadenitis (SDA), are leading causes of respiratory symptoms. (None of these organisms is infectious to humans.) Rats also can acquire a strep infection, which is usually fatal within three days unless treated. A strep infection can be transmitted from people to rats, so anyone with strep throat should stay away from rats.

If your rat starts sleeping more than usual, call your veterinarian.

This rat's abnormal coordination suggests that she has a pituitary tumor.

A respiratory infection often invades the inner ear. This throws off the rat's balance, causing his head to tilt to one side. Prompt treatment with antibiotics and steroids can usually reverse the symptoms. If treatment is delayed, the symptoms can progress until the rat walks in a circle or rolls over and over, and permanent damage to the rat's sense of balance can result. A rat with severely impaired balance has trouble eating and drinking and may need to be euthanized.

Tumors are the second most common cause of death in rats, especially in females. Tumors can be either benign (non-cancerous) or malignant (cancerous). Benign tumors can grow as fast as malignant tumors, but they often can be removed by surgery. Contrary to popular belief, rats are no more prone to cancer than any other animal. The symptoms of cancer include a skin ulcer, bleeding from a lump, a persistent abscess, a distended abdomen, weight loss, and lethargy.

The most common tumors found in rats are benign mammary and pituitary tumors. The most effective way to prevent tumors in females is to have them spayed. (Males are less prone to tumors.) You could also try to locate a breeder who has been selectively eliminating the tendency for tumors from his or her stock.

Not all lumps are tumors. Many lumps found on rats are abscesses. Abscesses are infections commonly caused by small bite or scratch wounds from another rat. They are usually within the skin, which means the skin is attached firmly to the lump.

An abscess usually requires treatment with oral antibiotics, and you should consult your veterinarian. Any abscess or pus in the area of the jaw or mouth should be suspected as a tooth abscess, a serious condition in a rat.

Bumblefoot is a bacterial infection in the bottom of the heel caused by irritation. It usually appears as a round, reddish swelling that eventually forms a yellowish crusty scab, which sometimes breaks open and bleeds. The best treatment is preventive treatment. Eliminate the source of the problem by removing wire floors in the cage or covering them with either Magic Mat made by Oasis (available at pet stores) or a plastic needlepoint canvas. Both are easy to remove for cleaning and can be cut to fit the floor exactly. The rat may be sensitive to his litter or bedding. You can try different types, use a litter box to keep the cage floor free of litter, or use towels instead. An overweight rat should be put on a diet to reduce the pressure on his feet.

Injuries and infections of the eye are fairly common in rats. Watery eyes are commonly caused by infection and foreign objects, such as ingrown hairs. An injury to the cornea will

Covering the floor wires of your rats' cage with a mat can prevent bumblefoot.

appear as a white "scar" on the surface of the eye. This should not be confused with a cataract, which appears as a white dot behind the pupil. There is no treatment for cataracts in rats, and while cataracts do cause blindness, they are not painful. Blindness in rats is only a little handicap, since they rely heavily on their senses of smell, hearing, and touch. House a blind rat in a one-story cage, and always keep furnishings in the same place.

Hair loss can be caused by excessive scratching, a fungal infection such as ringworm, or hormone problems. Rex or velour rats can lose hair as they age or as a result of stress or disease. Bald spots could be caused by barbering.

The Weekly Home Health Exam

Rats are so small that many medical procedures are difficult or impossible to perform on them. For this reason, it is important that health problems are discovered early and treated promptly. A weekly home exam takes only a few minutes and could save your rat's life. A daily exam should be done on sick rats to quickly identify any new problems.

Spend some time observing your rats both in and out of the cage so you'll know their normal behavior, appearance, gait, and activity level and so you'll be able to notice any changes. Rats gradually become less active as they age. A sudden reduction in activity is a common sign of disease. Pay special attention to each rat's breathing pattern. Heaving sides or noise made while breathing are symptoms of advanced respiratory infection or heart disease.

Start the exam by rubbing the rat around the head and neck to relax him. As you rub, feel for scabs or abnormal lumps. Massage the rest of the body, paying particular attention to the armpits and groin where tumors are common. The first time you do an exam on your rat, feel the coat to learn its normal texture, and pinch a small amount of skin so you know how thick the skin normally feels. Then each time you do an exam, check the coat and skin for any changes. A change in coat texture or the thickness of the skin can be a symptom of disease.

Check your rat's hydration status by gently pulling up a pinch of skin on his back and letting it go. Normally, the skin falls back in place quickly. If the skin returns slowly, your rat may be dehydrated and needs to see a vet. The toes, nose, and tail tip (unless the rat is dark) should be pink. Gently pull the rat's lips back to check that the teeth are straight and the normal length, and while you're there,

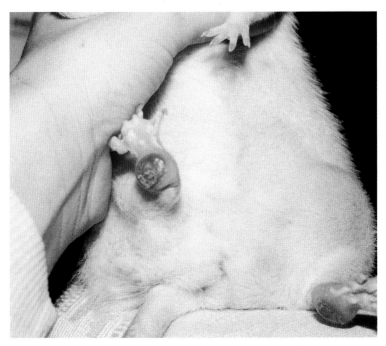

Bumblefoot is a preventable infection in the bottom of a foot.

make sure the tongue and gums are pink. Smell the breath coming from his nose, and check his ears for any bad odor or dark matter inside. A bad smell from the nose or ears can indicate an infection.

Look carefully at the rat's eyes for squinting, cloudiness, or swelling of the eyelids. A brownish-red discharge from the nose or eyes, or red matter caked around these areas means your rat's eyes have been running. Rats have a red pigment called porphyrin that is present in their tears. If the eyes water, porphyrin can be deposited around the eyes or nose in globs or crusts. It can also be spread to the arms, neck, and ears. Porphyrin deposits are sometimes mistaken for blood. A small amount of porphyrin is nothing to worry about, but large deposits may indicate an eye problem or respiratory infection.

Carefully examine your rat on a weekly basis, taking note of any changes.

Check the rat's toenails to see that they aren't too long, and check the bottoms of the back feet for bumblefoot sores, which require treatment. Now look at the rat's tail and hind end for any discharge or other abnormalities. Try to see a drop of urine from the urethra to check for blood. Normal urine is yellow. A female rat does not have a period, and any discharge from the vagina is a symptom of a uterine disease.

Parasites

Domestic rats can carry parasites such as pinworm, tapeworm, and a bladder threadworm, but the parasites rarely cause health problems. If your rat has persistent diarrhea, take a fecal sample to your veterinarian to be examined.

External parasites such as lice, mites, and fleas are a more common problem. Rat lice (*Polyplax spinulosa*) are tiny and best seen with a magnifying glass. Yellow to reddish brown and cigar shaped, lice are most commonly found on a rat's back. The eggs, or nits, of the lice appear as a silvery coating on the fur.

There are two mites common in rats. The tropical rat mite (*Ornithonyssus bacoti*) looks like a tiny tick. It lives in cracks around the rat's cage and crawls on the rat only to suck blood. It also bites humans. The microscopic fur mite (*Radfordia ensifera*) lives in hair follicles and can cause intense itching. Neither rat lice nor fur mites can live on people or other animals, and human lice can't live on rats.

The most effective and safest treatment for lice and mites is ivermectin (also good for internal parasites) given orally. Have all your rats treated, and clean and disinfect the cage and bedding to eliminate any fallen eggs. If your rats have tropical rat

Above: The reddish areas surrounding the nose are caused by porphyrin deposits.
Below: Louse nits (the eggs) can be seen as a whitish covering on the fur. Also watch for excessive scratching.

mites, you'll also need to treat areas near their cage—where the wall meets the floor, for instance—with a pesticide. Dog and cat fleas are also happy to live on your rats. Treat your rats using a product designed for rodents or cats. Also treat your dog or cat, house, and yard.

To prevent external parasites, check new rats carefully before introducing them to your resident rats. Don't use food, litter, or bedding that has been stored open near other rats, since the items may harbor lice or mites.

Dental Care

It's a myth that a rat's teeth overgrow unless he has something hard to chew on. Normally, the upper and lower teeth line up and keep each other sharp and the proper length by grinding together. Overgrown teeth can occur only if the teeth are misaligned or broken off, there is nerve or muscle damage in the jaw, or there is a tooth abscess. Disease of the teeth or jaw can prevent a rat from eating hard foods.

Rat teeth don't contain nerves, so trimming them is painless to your pet (although the gums sometimes bleed slightly). The teeth should be trimmed whenever it looks like they are long enough to irritate the mouth or cause difficulty eating. This may be every one to three weeks, depending on the problem. Dog toenail or human fingernail clippers work best, or your vet can trim your rat's teeth.

Right: Enlist the help of a friend if you choose to trim your rat's teeth yourself.

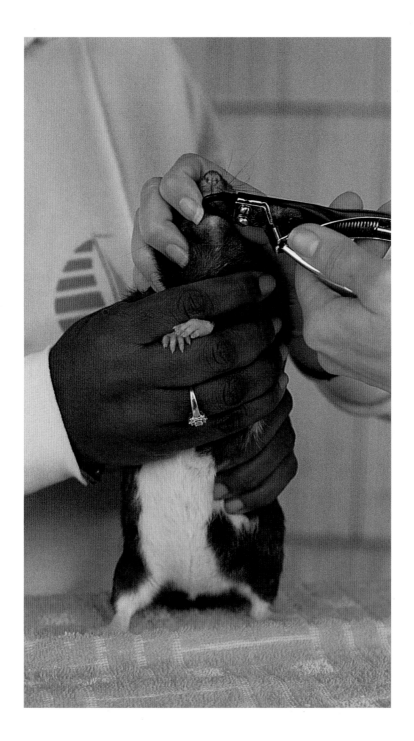

Trimming Teeth

To trim a rat's teeth, it's best if one person holds your rat while a second person does the dental work. You can wrap your rat tightly in a towel to restrict his movements. The clippers should be angled so that the tooth retains its original bevel (look at another rat's teeth for reference). Top teeth should be clipped to a length of $1/4$ inch, bottom teeth to $1/2$ inch. Be very careful to hold the lips out of the way and make sure the tongue is also out of the way before clipping. After snapping off, the teeth will have jagged edges. If your rat is cooperative, you might try filing his teeth with a nail file. Otherwise, give him bones to chew on to help smooth his teeth.

Health Problems of Older Rats

The most common health problems seen in aging rats are tumors and infections, which have already been discussed, paraplegia, strokes, and kidney and heart degeneration.

Paraplegia, which usually has a gradual onset, is often the result of nerve degeneration in the rat's spine. There is no known cause or treatment, but most rats get along just fine with some paralysis and do not seem to suffer. A paraplegic rat needs soft food (rat blocks can be soaked in water) and may need grooming, and his ears and genitals cleaned.

Common signs of kidney disease are increased drinking and urination. Other diseases can cause these symptoms, so lab tests are required for diagnosis. If your vet determines your rat would benefit from even more fluid intake, you can add juice to the water to encourage drinking.

Symptoms of heart failure are similar to those of respiratory disease and can include tiredness, lack of appetite, and edema (fluid retention) of the skin, which makes the skin puffy and can be mistaken for excess fat. In advanced cases, the toenails can turn blue from lack of oxygen. Congestive heart failure seems to be fairly common and causes edema of the skin. Congestive heart failure can be successfully treated with a diuretic, a beta-blocker, an ACE inhibitor, and sometimes digitoxin. Consult your vet.

The most common symptom of a stroke in rats is sudden paralysis, especially on just one side of the body. A vet will recommend immediate treatment with anti-inflammatories, such as steroids. A stroke is not painful, and rats often recover. During recovery, you may have to help your rat eat, and gentle physical therapy may be beneficial.

First Aid

The most common injuries in rats are minor scratches and lacerations inflicted by other rats. The body skin of rats contains few pain receptors, and wounds usually bleed little and heal quickly. Unless the wound is large enough to require stitches (over 1 inch long), all that's necessary is to apply a topical antibiotic to prevent infection. Also, keep the cage spotlessly clean and replace the litter with rags or paper.

If your rat takes a fall or is stepped on, the treatment depends on the severity of the injury. Minor injuries such as bruises or sprains usually heal on their own. Rats are pretty tough, but fractures and internal injuries can occur. If your rat appears to have a serious injury or seems lethargic, rush him to the vet.

Rats can catch a leg in the cage wire. This usually occurs

in cages made of 1-inch x ½-inch mesh, which is why that size is not recommended. If you witness such an injury, apply a cold compress to help prevent swelling. If the leg appears to be broken or if the swelling does not go down by the next day, take your rat to the veterinarian.

Since the feet, ears, and tail all have a considerable blood supply, injuries to these areas can cause profuse bleeding. The first step in stopping the bleeding is to apply gentle, direct pressure for two minutes. If the bleeding continues, try holding ice against the injury. If you cannot stop the bleeding, rush your rat to the veterinarian.

A toenail bleeds if broken off or cut too short. The best way to control the bleeding is to press styptic powder or a silver nitrate stick into the end of the nail. Flour or cornstarch can also be used.

Heatstroke is a condition that requires immediate treat-

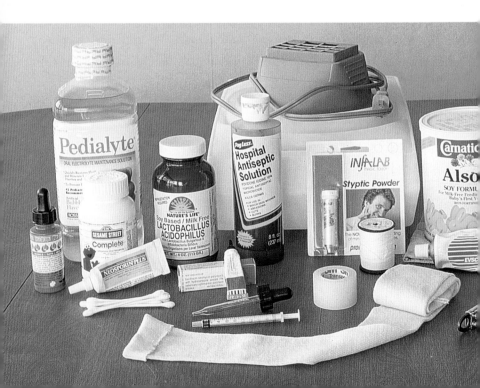

ment. The symptoms of heatstroke can include drooling, lethargy, or unconsciousness. The tail will feel quite warm. Immediately cool the rat by submerging him up to his neck in cool water. Also encourage him to drink an electrolyte beverage, such as Pedialyte or Gatorade, or water containing a pinch of sugar and salt. If your rat doesn't recover quickly, rush him to the vet.

If a rat appears to be choking, he probably has something stuck in his throat. Because of the arrangement of the rat's throat, true choking, which interferes with breathing, is rare. Food stuck in the throat can cause gagging and drooling, but as long as your rat can breathe, there is nothing you can do other than try to comfort him. If it does seem like your rat is having trouble breathing, rush him to the vet.

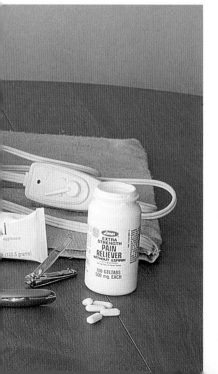

A medical kit containing first aid and nursing supplies will prepare you for both emergencies and caring for sick rats.

Preventing Heatstroke

BECAUSE RATS ARE NOCTURNAL, THEY HAVEN'T EVOLVED TO ENDURE HEAT. A rat's cage should be kept indoors where temperature can be controlled. For healthy rats, temperatures above 90° F are uncomfortable, above 100° F can cause distress, and above 104° F can be fatal. Rats use their tails as heat releasers, sending more blood to the skin surface to help radiate excess body heat. You can tell how warm a rat is by feeling the tail. Tailless rats or rats with health problems, especially respiratory infections, are even more temperature sensitive. Use special care if you take your rats outside on a hot day or if you plan to travel with them during hot weather. Rats should never be left in the sun or left unattended in a vehicle.

During hot weather, if you do not have air-conditioning, you'll need to take special precautions to keep your rats cool. Keep a thermometer near their cage to measure the temperature. Draw the drapes and close the windows during the day; only open them at night. Put the cage on the floor in the coolest room of the house—usually the bathroom—or maybe even put it in the bathtub, and run a fan in the room to circulate the air.

Freeze water in a plastic bottle, close the lid tight, and put it in the cage, or use a jar filled with ice cubes. You can also offer your rats treats of frozen fruits and vegetables to help them cool off. If it gets really hot and one of your rats seems miserable, dunk him in cool water up to his neck.

Nursing Care

The goal of nursing care is to administer necessary medications and maintain the patient's comfort, hygiene, nutrition, and spirits in order to support healing. Because rats are so small, they require some special nursing techniques.

Rats usually accept liquid medicine if it tastes good. Giving rats bitter medication can be a struggle. Bitter medications are often accepted more readily as a powder (from capsules or crushed tablets) mixed in food such as mashed avocado or baby food.

Keep a rat who is convalescing warm and his environment clean. For a rat with a respiratory infection, run a humidifier in the room. A sick rat will usually eat and drink more if you offer him food and water by hand. An excellent supplement for a sick or underweight rat is human baby soy formula. Give a sick rat one to two scoops of powdered formula mixed with water and rodent vitamins daily. Be sure to hold and talk to your rat patient to keep his spirits up.

Surgical Care

There are a few things you should know before your veterinarian schedules your rat for surgery. An overnight fast is standard procedure for cats and dogs to prevent vomiting while under anesthesia. Rats can't vomit, though, so an overnight fast is unnecessary. In fact, because rats have such a fast metabolism and eat most of their food at night, an overnight fast depletes their energy resources. You should, however, withhold food and water two hours before the surgery. Also, rats are prone to hypothermia and must be kept warm during and after surgery.

Only inhalational anesthetics such as isoflurane should be used on rats so the level of anesthesia can be carefully controlled. Injectable anesthetics can be dangerous for rats.

About 10 percent of rats who have had surgery chew out their sutures, probably because of pain or discomfort. An analgesic is recommended. The incision can be protected with a taped body cast or a cervical collar. An Elizabethan collar is not recommended for rats because it can prevent eating, drinking, and grooming.

After the surgery, check the incision daily for problems. Normal healing may cause some swelling, redness, and scabs, but pus, drainage, greenish skin, or a bad smell means infection, and you should contact your vet for instructions.

Rat Health Care

FOR MORE DETAILED INFORMATION ON RAT health care, the Rat Health Care booklet, published by The Rat Fan Club, is a good source. To order a copy, contact The Rat Fan Club, listed in Appendix 2 on page 181. You may want to pass the information on to your vet or offer to purchase a copy if he or she expresses interest in learning more about rat health care.

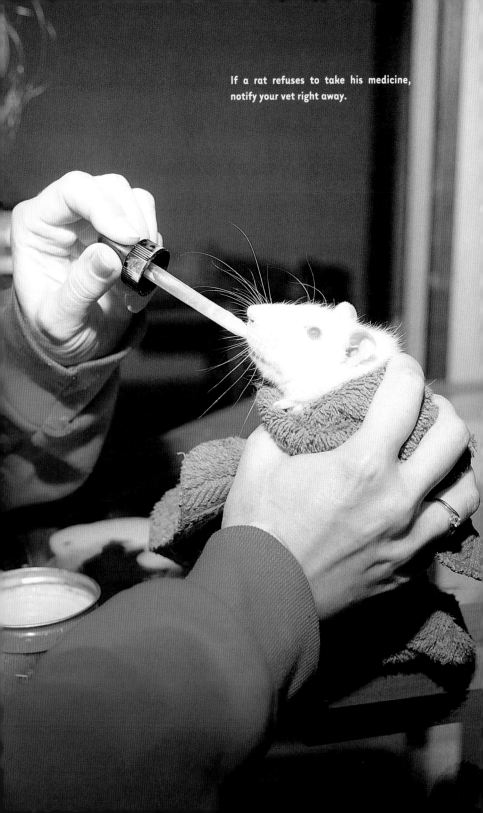

If a rat refuses to take his medicine, notify your vet right away.

CHAPTER

7

Fun Activities
to Do with Your Rats

Teaching your rat to sit up is a good stepping stone to teaching other, more complicated tricks.

Rats love to play and explore. They are intelligent and enjoy the stimulation of outings, learning how to play games, and performing tricks. There are a lot of fun indoor and outdoor games you can play with your rats. Rats outside enjoy running in the grass, climbing bushes, and digging in the dirt. Rats especially enjoy picnics because of the food! Some rats like to play in water. If you start when they're young, you can even teach your rats to enjoy swimming (hairless rats do not float well, however). You might want to equip your rats with a harness and light leash for outdoor excursions. Harnesses designed for ferrets, rabbits, or iguanas fit all but the tiniest of rats.

Watch out for dangerous outdoor elements. Spiders and insects that bite or sting, poisonous plants, fertilizers and pesticides, and neighborhood cats can harm your rats. Don't let your rats play where wild mice or rats might live such as under buildings, in barns, or near sewers. Wild rodents carry diseases and parasites your rats can catch. Also, don't take your rats outside on extremely hot or cold days, and don't leave them under very bright sun.

Because rats are social, most of them enjoy meeting new people and accompanying their owners almost everywhere they go. Your rats can ride on your shoulder, in a hip pack, or in a special pouch. But don't take your rats into buildings where animals aren't allowed, such as restaurants, or to places where the noise and lights might be frightening to your rats, such as parties, bars, concerts, theaters, or parks with firework displays. Just use your common sense.

It's a good idea to expose your rats to a variety of experiences when they're young and adaptable so that when they're older, new experiences and changes won't be as stressful. The more experiences rats have, the calmer they will be in all kinds of situations. Stress can make animals more susceptible to disease, so by socializing your rats as much as possible when they're young, you could be improving their health later on. You and your rats can have a lot of fun together!

A harness provides extra security on outdoor adventures.

Games to Play with Your Rat

Rats are smart enough to learn all kinds of games. By playing with your rats, you will increase the bonds between you and your rats and stimulate their brains, which can increase your rats' intelligence! Always keep in mind that rats are small animals and can be easily injured. If you play a game where your rats are on the floor, be careful not to step on them, and always take your shoes off.

Rats enjoy crawling through finger tunnels, especially if the tunnels are provided by their favorite people.

Making finger tunnels is an easy, safe way for children to play with rats. To make a finger tunnel, form a circle with your thumb and fingers. You can make it twice as wide by using both hands, or make it twice as long by putting one hand behind the other. You can also make a tunnel by spreading your thumb and fingers apart and resting the tips on a surface with your hand forming an arch. Lead a rat through the tunnel with a treat. Once she learns the game, you probably won't need to use treats. Try leading a rat around by putting tunnels in front of her one after another.

Rats are partially predatory and like to chase small moving objects. By moving objects like string, rubber bands, feathers, strips of paper, small crumpled paper balls, and loose springs (the spiral wire from a calendar or notebook works well), you can interest a rat in chasing them. For safety reasons, don't let your rats play with string or rubber bands by themselves.

Some rats really enjoy the crackling noise made by paper bags. Open a small bag and lay it on its side. To get your rats' attention, rustle the bag with your hand or scratch on the side of it. Your rats may enjoy running in and out of the bag, pouncing on it, or sitting in the bag while you gently shake it and pull it around. A paper bag can be put in your rats' cage or playground as a toy, but avoid plastic bags, which could cause suffocation.

Another game can help you explore a rat's intelligence. Show one of your rats a treat and hide it in your hand while she watches. Say, "Which hand?" and hold out your fists with the fingers up. When your rat picks the correct hand by sniffing or prying at your fingers, give her the treat. If she picks the wrong hand, open it to show her the treat isn't there and encourage her to go to the other hand.

If it seems like your rat remembers which hand she saw you put the treat in (instead of just guessing or smelling it), try hiding your hands behind your back briefly (but don't switch the treat) to see if she still remembers the correct hand.

When you have developed a strong bond with your rats, you can try playing hide-and-seek. Start by picking an easy hiding place, such as behind a chair or doorway. Call your rats' names, saying, "Come find me." If your rats seem confused, step out of the hiding place, call them, and then hide again. Once they find you easily in one room, you can start hiding in other rooms.

You can hide treats and have your rats search for them in a treasure hunt. You can hide one treat at a time or several. You can play with one rat or several. To start, show your rats where you hide each treat. As they learn the game, you can hide the treats in more difficult locations. Letting your rats watch you hide the treats tests their powers of observation and memory. Hiding the treats when they're not watching tests their powers of exploration.

For another game involving one rat and her favorite treats, pick two foods making sure one is your rat's favorite. Teach her their names by saying the word every time you give her the food and repeat the name while she eats. You can test your rat's food preferences and knowledge with the help of another person. Each person holds one of the two foods. Put your rat between you and have each person repeat the name of the food in hand. If your rat really understands the words, she should run to the person who has her favorite food. Reward her with a piece of the food. Then try again, only this time switch foods. That way you'll know if your rat is really choosing her favorite food or her favorite person! Once your rat knows the game, you can try other foods or activities.

Through chasing moving objects during play, rats can exercise their predatory instinct.

Demonstrating that your rat understands words is an impressive trick to show friends.

Rats can learn the meanings of words, so if you name each game and say the name of the game before you play it, eventually your rats will recognize the word and know what game you want to play. If a rat doesn't want to play, it might be because she isn't in the mood to play, doesn't like the game, or is feeling insecure. Respect her wishes. A shy rat may feel more secure playing with you while she's in her cage, inside a box or tube, or under a cloth. If a rat doesn't like one game, there are plenty of other fun games to play. We've provided only a sampling.

This fawn-colored rat is playing hide-and-seek.

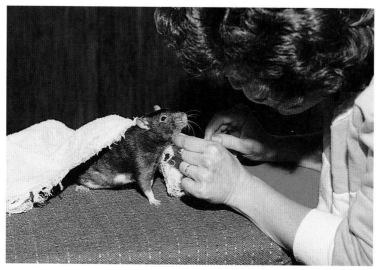

Above: For fun, you can put your rat under a cloth, then tickle and play with her.
Right: Teaching your rat to climb a rope is fun for both you and the rat.

Tricks to Teach Your Rats

Animals, including humans, tend to repeat behaviors that are rewarded. This principle is called positive reinforcement and is the method used to teach tricks. Food is the most common reward used to teach tricks. A cereal such as Rice Krispies works well because each piece is so small you can give a rat a lot of it before she gets full.

To teach a trick you need to break it into steps. You teach one step at a time, with each step requiring the rat to do a little more to receive the reward. Each rat will learn at a different pace. For some rats you may only need to do each step once. For others you may need to repeat each step several times. If your rat seems confused during the training, go back one or two steps. It takes a lot of practice before a rat really understands a trick.

A rat needs to be in the right mood to learn a trick. If she doesn't respond, try again later. It's usually best to work with one rat at a time when teaching a trick, although competition from another rat can sometimes encourage a lazy rat.

Teaching a rat to sit up is a good way for her to begin learning basic commands. Hold a treat above the rat's head. Say her name and the word *up*. You may have to show her the treat and lift it slowly. At first, reward her for any attempt to sit up. Then require that she sit up taller and taller. Eventually, your rat might sit up on command without the treat over her head.

Like all companion rats, this rat is always ready for a fun game.

You can teach your rat to walk in a circle. Give her the command *turn* and use a treat to lead her around in a circle. As soon as she completes a circle, give her the food and praise her. Gradually hold your hand up higher and farther away from her. As long as your rat continues to make the circle, you can start abbreviating the hand motion until eventually, you signal your rat to turn just by moving your hand briefly to the right or left. Just don't practice so much your rat gets dizzy!

A fun and more challenging trick is the rope climb. Wrap heavy string around the top of a table and tie it to a piece of heavy rope so that the rope hangs down from the edge of the table. Set something heavy such as a brick or book on the end of the rope to hold it taut. Put your rat on the book, and hold a treat above her head next to the rope. You want your rat to stand on her hind legs to reach for the treat. When she grabs the rope for support, give her the treat. Next, hold a treat a bit higher and try to get her to start climbing the rope. Continue to reward your rat whenever she grabs the rope, and each time hold the treat a little higher.

Your rat should catch on fairly quickly and start to climb the rope. The first time she does so, give her the treat immediately and fuss over her. The next time, make her climb an inch or so higher before giving her the treat. Gradually ask her to climb higher and higher before giving her the treat. Eventually, she'll climb all the way to the top.

Another trick employing a rope is the tightrope walk. The secret to this trick is to get the rope taut. The tighter and thicker the rope, the easier it is for your rat to walk across it. Tie the rope between two table legs (you might have to tape it in place to keep it from sliding down) at chair height with two chairs as the platforms. Put pillows or a large folded blanket underneath the tightrope in case your rat falls.

Place your rat on one of the platforms and give her a few treats so she feels comfortable there. Then try leading her onto the rope with a treat. If your rat refuses to venture onto the rope, place her on the tightrope a short distance from the end so that she faces a platform. Once she learns how to balance on the rope, she may be more willing to start from the platform. Your rat needs to learn both skill and self-confidence in walking the tightrope, so don't rush the learning process. Let her learn at her own pace.

Here is a rewarding trick that's fun to watch. Put your rat on a table or on the top of her cage. Fasten a piece of string so it hangs down over the edge of the table or cage. Make sure the surface where your rat will be standing has good footing: you don't want your rat to slip and fall while pulling on the string. Fasten a small Dixie cup to the string with a paper clip and put a treat in the cup. Start with the cup hanging down within reach of the rat and let her remove the treat from it. Next, add another treat to the cup, and move the cup down slightly so she has to reach down to pull it up. Give the rat the command *pull it up*. As you repeat the exercise and move the cup lower on the string, encourage your rat to pull the string up to get the treat. Pull on the string yourself to show your rat how to do it. It may take some time for her to get the idea and learn the best pulling technique.

These fun games and tricks help stimulate your rats' brains, increase communication skills, and allow you and your rats to interact on a playful level. Playing helps develop a bonding and enriching relationship.

Rats are intelligent and coordinated and therefore are capable of performing tricks such as pulling up a treat-filled cup attached to a string.

CHAPTER

8

Showing Your Rats

A judge evaluates a show rat.

A GROWING NUMBER OF PEOPLE ENJOY SHOWING THEIR rats. Most rat clubs hold shows, and new club chapters are popping up in different parts of the United States. If a club or chapter does not yet exist in your area, perhaps you can help organize one! To start a club all you need is a group of people who are interested and motivated. Contact an already existing show club for help. The Rat and Mouse Club of America, which is based in Los Angeles, has been particularly active in supporting chapters in other parts of the U.S.

Before deciding to show your rats, familiarize yourself with club rules and standards. Each club has its own rules and interpretations of what constitutes the "perfect" rat. A rat entered in the wrong category may be disqualified. Don't hesitate to ask for help with filling out the entry form.

There are two basic types of classes at a rat show—pet and variety. In the pet classes, rats are judged by how friendly, clean, and healthy they are. The judge picks a winner based on the rat he or she feels would make the best companion—color and variety are irrelevant.

Variety classes have more categories of judgement. In the variety classes, rats are judged on the five C's: color, conformation, coat, condition, and character (temperament). Most clubs have separate categories for smooth-coated (standard), rex, and odd-eyed rats. They may also have separate categories for tailless, hairless, and Dumbo, where more points are awarded for physical features and fewer for color. The following descriptions of color are based on the show standards published by some of the rodent clubs.

This tailless rat has a flecked coloring, called agouti.

Color in rats can be divided into three basic types: self, ticked, and shaded. Self-colored rats are all one color with each hair the same color from base to tip. The albino, which lacks pigment other than the red blood protein hemoglobin, fits into this category and is called pink-eyed white. There is also a black-eyed white, which is more difficult to breed.

The ticked color types all originated from the wild rat color, called agouti. Each hair has bands of color causing a flecked or shimmering effect, and the belly is always lighter than the rest of the body. In agouti, for instance, the main hairs have a slate gray base and a chestnut tip. Some of the longer, protective guard hairs are black, and the belly is a light gray. Overall, an agouti rat looks brown but is actually brown, black, and gray.

The shaded group includes Himalayan and Siamese colors. A Himalayan rat is white with colored points (ears, nose, feet, tail), while the Siamese is more of a cream or light beige that gradually fades into the points. The colored points are temperature sensitive and only develop on areas of the body that are coolest.

A rat of any color, even an albino rat, can carry genes that cause white markings. When Siamese or Himalayan rats have white markings, their colored points can be wiped out by the white, which is very undesirable for show animals. In rats there is a series of genes that cause varying amounts of white on the body. Some genes produce white only on the belly, legs, and tail. Some genes produce more widespread white markings resulting in rats who are hooded or rats who have only small spots of color. White markings can vary considerably, and it is a challenge for breeders to produce rats who match show standards.

BEST
KITTEN

Most clubs call baby rats kittens,
though the scientific term for baby rats
is pups.

Preparing a Rat for a Show

Although it can be fun to enter a rat in a show, there are a couple of things you should keep in mind. A show can be stressful for a rat. Shows generally last all day and may involve traveling. Hot weather makes the experience even more difficult for the rat. Find out if the show building will be air-conditioned. In addition, there is the risk of the rat being exposed to disease, so if some of your rats have been to a show, it's a good idea to quarantine them for two weeks. You should decide if the benefits of taking a rat to a show outweigh the risks. You may decide it is just as fun to attend the show without your rats.

You shouldn't choose just any rat to enter in a show. Don't put your rat through the stress of a show unless he is particularly suited for competition. A show rat should have an outgoing personality. Shy or nervous rats won't have fun. If you want to enter your rat in a variety class, he should come close to meeting the club's standards. A rat who doesn't fit any of the standards will be disqualified. In addition, any rat who is sick, deformed (including a kinked tail), missing body parts (including whiskers or part of an ear), pregnant, nursing, or in poor condition will also be disqualified.

Once you're sure your rat meets the requirements for entering a show, be sure to send in your entry form by the deadline. Begin preparing your rat at least a week ahead of time. He should be squeaky clean, so you might need to give him a bath. This should be done about a week before the show to give the coat time after the bath to regain its natural oils and shine. Be sure to scrub his tail. Before bathing your rat, clean the cage so you won't put him back in a dirty environment.

Above: This shiny rat is called a black satin. *Below:* This chinchilla blaze Berkshire rat (front) and agouti rat (back) can compete in the variety competition of a rat show.

You can add a few extra sunflower seeds to your rat's diet a week before the show. The extra oil and vitamins will help put a nice sheen on his coat. Two days before the show, clip his toenails. This is required and is a courtesy to the judges to help prevent them from getting scratched.

Most clubs require that a rat be brought to the show table in a special type of cage. Some clubs have these show boxes for rent. Make sure you have a clean show box and clean bedding to show off your rat to his best advantage. Your rat should ride to the show in his regular travel cage.

Bathing Your Rat

Baby shampoo or any shampoo safe for cats is safe for rats. For white rats, a bluing shampoo, designed to make whites whiter, is recommended. For an intact male with a very greasy back, you might want to first use cold cream or ½ teaspoon of Dawn dishwashing liquid (the best grease cutter) mixed in ¼ cup of water to remove the grease before bathing.

Fill a sink or dish pan with warm water deep enough to reach your rat's neck. Get your rat wet, then set him on a towel while you rub in the shampoo. It's not necessary to wash his face, and try not to get water in his eyes or ears. To rinse, lower him back down into the water and rub him thoroughly to remove all the shampoo. Then towel dry your rat and let him lick off the rest of the water if the weather is warm. If the air is cold, you can use a blow-dryer set on low, keeping it a foot away, and don't point it at your rat's face.

To wash your rat's tail, bundle him tightly in a hand towel by placing him in the center and folding half of the towel over his face. Then quickly fold the ends of the towel around the rat, leaving his tail hanging out the bottom. The tighter you wrap your rat, the calmer he will be. On either side of the base of your rat's tail, pinch the ends of towel together and fasten with safety pins, being careful not to stick your rat. Gently scrub the tail with shampoo, warm water, and a soft toothbrush, then rinse. If your rat struggles, do only a little at a time to avoid stressing him too much.

Clipping Your Rat's Nails

TRIMMING YOUR RAT'S TOENAILS IS REALLY QUITE EASY TO DO ONCE BOTH you and the rat are used to it. The best tool is a pair of human fingernail clippers. To clip the back toenails hold your rat on your lap facing left if you're right-handed (right if you're left-handed). Press him against your stomach with your left forearm (right forearm if left-handed) to hold him still, and hold his foot in your left hand (right hand if left-handed). Pull his foot backward and clip the nails with your other hand. To clip your rat's fingernails, use the same method but face your rat in the opposite direction and pull your rat's hand forward instead of backward.

You need to clip off only the sharp tip at the end of the nail. If you cut off too much, the nail will bleed. It's a good idea to have some styptic powder or silver nitrate sticks on hand to stop any bleeding, but if you're careful, bleeding rarely occurs. You can eliminate the chance of accidentally cutting a toe by holding the foot so only the nails stick out. Your fingers protect the toes.

If your rat really struggles, do only a few nails at a time. Reward him with a treat afterward. You can also distract him during the procedure by giving him a treat in the beginning.

Keep your rat's face dry when bathing him.

At the Show

You should arrive at least a half hour before the rat portion of the show begins (most clubs also judge mice and sometimes hamsters), so you have time to check in, get your paperwork, make any necessary changes, pick up any show boxes you are renting, and present your rats for the health exam. Rats who appear sick are not allowed to compete in the show and neither are their cage mates. You'll be given an ID card to be placed on each rat's show box. Do not allow other people to handle your rats unless they first disinfect their hands.

Before a rat's class is called, you may groom the rat to remove loose hairs and dust. Many competitors use a shaving brush or silk

This silver mink is sitting on his paperwork for a show.

cloth. When the class is called, carry the show box to the show table and place it where instructed. Once the rat is placed on the judging table, you may not touch him or indicate which rat is yours. This rule is to help ensure the judge's decision won't be influenced. While the judging is going on, by all means observe, but do not talk loudly, and do not talk to the judge or make any remarks that may tell him or her which rat is yours. If you have questions, the judge will be happy to talk to you after the judging is over for the day. The clerk will let you know when you may claim your rat. If he is a winner, he may still be in competition, so do not approach him or let anyone know he is yours until you have the permission of the clerk.

Finally, be a good sport. The purpose of the show is to have fun, meet other rat people, and see other rats—not just to win.

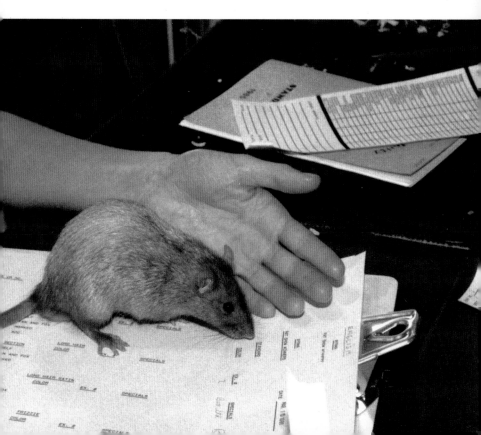

CHAPTER

9

Breeding Rats

Breeding stock should be carefully chosen according to age, temperament, health, and appearance in order to produce quality offspring.

RATS ARE EASY TO BREED. IN FACT, MANY OWNERS END up with rats having unplanned pups. This is because domesticated rats reach puberty as early as five weeks of age. Brothers and sisters, and even mothers and sons, must be separated before the youngsters reach this age.

The decision to breed rats is a serious one and commits you to a big responsibility. The purpose should be to produce healthy, well-socialized rats who have great personalities and will make good companions. The average litter size for domestic rats is twelve pups. It takes effort to find good homes for all the pups. As rats become more popular, homes may be easier to find, but rats are still being found in animal shelters. Don't add more rats to the overpopulation problem.

You may be able to sell your pups to a pet shop, but keep in mind most pet shops sell 50 to 90 percent of their rats for reptile food. If you're lucky, you might be able to find a pet shop that is willing to sell your rats only as pets. You could also advertise your rats for sale in the newspaper or in animal newsletters or magazines. If there is a rodent club in your area, it is beneficial to join. Most clubs have a newsletter and allow you to advertise your rats, and some allow you to sell rats at shows.

When advertising your rats, make it clear that your rats are to be pets only, and screen the applicants to make sure they will provide a good home for your babies. Recommend they buy books on rat care so they'll know how to care for their new rats. Try not to sell a rat who'll live alone as a single rat.

Responsible breeders keep in touch with their rats' new families to see how the rats are doing. Make sure buyers understand that if they can no longer take care of their rats, you will take them back. Staying informed about the rats you sell also helps you plan your breeding program because you'll know if your rats develop health problems later in life.

A responsible breeder takes into account each rat's individual characteristics and age. You should never breed a rat who has had symptoms of a respiratory infection. Many people have bred rats with active mycoplasmosis, and that is one of the main reasons this disease has become so common.

The best age to breed a female for the first time is when she is four to five months old. Never breed a female rat for the first time if she is older than eight months. If she hasn't given birth by that age, her pelvic canal will be fused in a narrow position, putting her at risk of not being able to deliver her pups normally. In such a case, a cesarean section may be necessary to save her life.

Above: A female rat in heat takes an active role in the mating process, some-times even escaping her cage and finding her way into a male rat's cage.

Below: A hobby breeder has equipped this room to breed both rats and mice. Breeding cages for rats should be as large as possible.

Although a rat of the proper age generally has little problem giving birth, there is always the risk of complications. If your female rat is dear to you, then it is safer not to breed her. In fact, she may have a healthier, longer life if you have her spayed instead.

Finally, you should only breed rats who have outstanding personalities. Never breed a rat who is shy, nervous, or aggressive, since these behaviors tend to be genetic. It also doesn't hurt to breed a rat who is particularly beautiful. While health and personality are most important, appearance is also a factor. Let's face it, all things being equal, a beautiful rat may have a better chance of getting a home. If you're going to breed rats, you might as well breed individuals who are healthy, have great personalities, and are beautiful.

The equipment and space required to breed rats depends on whether you want just an occasional litter or if you want to become a hobby breeder. To breed the occasional litter, you need at least three cages, one for males, one for females, and a maternity cage. Most hobby breeders devote a whole room to their many rat cages, and the necessary food, litter, and equipment. It's a good idea to talk to an established hobby breeder about the necessary time and money commitment.

Responsible hobby breeders generally do not make money from breeding rats. You should approach breeding as a hobby, not a business. The main goals should be the satisfaction and enjoyment of producing wonderful rats and improving the quality of their health, temperament, and appearance—not making money.

Rat Reproduction

Females of breeding age come into heat all year-round, every four to five days, unless they're pregnant. The heat usually begins in the evening and lasts most of the night. Each female usually has a regular schedule that can be marked on the calendar, but the schedule can vary.

You can breed rats simply by putting a pair together for ten days, to ensure they are together through two heat cycles, but the female might pick a fight with the male. Putting the pair together only when the female is in heat is a better way to breed rats. This method works especially well if you're breeding your rat to a rat who belongs to someone else because the pair has to be together for only one evening.

You can usually tell when a rat is in heat by her behavior. Stroke her back and if she is in heat she will perform the mating dance. She may first dart forward or spin around, then she braces her legs stiffly, lifts her head and tail, and vibrates her ears. This display tells the male, and the breeder, she is ready for mating.

Usually the male must mount the female many times before completing the act, so mating continues for some time. It is possible, however, for a female to get pregnant from a single mounting. Even if the female is not in heat, a determined and persistent male can sometimes stimulate the female into heat, so keep your fertile males and females separate!

The gestation period is normally twenty-two days but can vary from twenty-one to twenty-three. Two weeks into the pregnancy the mother's abdomen starts expanding. As the due date approaches, you may be able to see the babies moving inside the mother. The mother's needs are simple: a nutritious diet, exercise, and extra bedding to build a nest a few days before the expected event.

Hormones can sometimes change a pregnant or nursing rat's personality. She may become more aggressive or less interested in playing. Once the pups are weaned, the mother rat usually regains her normal personality. It's also common for mother rats to have soft stools.

Domesticated Rat Facts at a Glance

Body temperature *99.5° to 100.6° F*

Heart rate *260 to 600 bpm*

Respiration rate *65 to 115 bpm*

Average weight *female: 7 to 12 oz; male: 14 to 20 oz*

Weight at birth *5 to 6 g*

Litter size *1 to 33, average 12*

Number of nipples *10 to 12*

Age eyes open *14 days*

Weaning age *4 to 6 weeks*

Age at puberty *5 weeks*

Estrus cycle *4 to 5 days*

Gestation period *21 to 23 days*

Postpartum estrus *within 24 hours*

Social lifestyle *large family groups*

Average life span *2 to 3 years*

Food consumption *0.7 to 1.5 oz/day (dry food)*

Water consumption *1 to 2 oz/day (dry food diet)*

Optimum room temperature *72° to 78° F*

Optimum humidity *50 percent*

Sight *moderate/near-sighted*

Sense of smell *excellent*

Hearing *superior/ultrasonic*

Average breeding life *female: 18 months; male: 24 months*

This five-day-old hooded rat pup has just started growing her fur, but her markings are already apparent.

The Birthing Process

A bloody discharge from the vagina signals the start of the birth process, which normally takes about an hour or two. If pups haven't arrived within three hours, take the mother to a vet. It is normal for mother rats to eat pups who are born dead, but it's better to remove them. Only if she is disturbed or malnutritioned will a rat eat her live young.

It's a good idea to examine the pups daily—handling will stimulate and socialize them—and it's fun to watch their fast development. Wait until the mother is off her nest, then remove her from the cage; some mothers rush to defend their pups if they squeak when handled. Don't worry about putting your scent on the pups since that won't cause the mother to reject them.

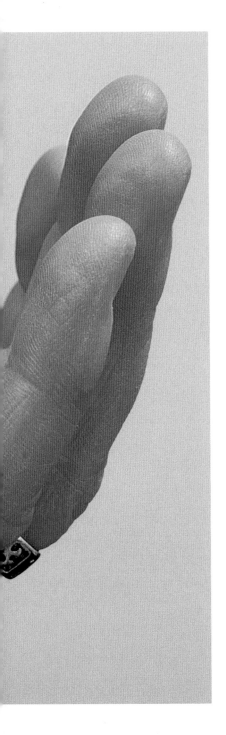

Occasionally, a mother will die or won't have enough milk. It is possible to hand raise rats, but it's very difficult. A better plan is to foster the pups to another nursing mother. A mother rat will almost always adopt other pups as long as they are about the same size as her own. If you don't have access to another nursing mother, check with other breeders or a pet shop.

Rats are born hairless and blind. Once they open their eyes, at fourteen days, you should play with the pups as much as possible. At this age they start eating their mother's food. By four to six weeks, the pups are ready to be weaned. If you plan to breed the mother a second time, wait a few weeks after her litter has been weaned to allow her to recover.

Rat pups grow quickly. This fourteen-day-old pup has just opened her eyes and will soon start leaving the nest to explore.

Sharing the Fun

There is no animal like a rat. Rats can be as intelligent, affectionate, playful, and personable as dogs and cats, but they also possess their own special charm. On one hand, rats can be stubborn and determined to get their own way, but on the other, they can be the most devoted and loyal companions. And of course, each rat is different, and each has a unique personality.

Talk to a few rat lovers, and you'll quickly realize that there is a special bond between rats and people. People who grow to love rats often say they never again want to be without pet rats in their house. Once you become acquainted with these wonderful little animals, your life may never be the same again!

Although rats are becoming more popular all the time, they still have a bad reputation with some people. Several rodent clubs and associations work to dispel myths and promote rats as companions. By joining one of these clubs, you can help support the efforts to educate people.

You will also benefit from being a club member by receiving information on new ways to play with your rats and how to keep them healthy. And you will be able to share your rat stories with others who will enjoy them. Many people who have rats say they feel isolated because they don't know anyone else with rats. These people appreciate the opportunity to communicate with fellow rat lovers through a club. We who love rats look forward to welcoming you to our group!

Rats are devoted, loyal pets that provide just as much campanionship as a dog or a cat.

Appendix 1

HEALTHY HOMEMADE RAT DIET

SERVING SIZES ARE FOR A 1-POUND RAT—ADJUST as necessary. For pups, add two extra servings of oyster or liver per week.

Daily

about 3 T molasses mix (*see recipe below*)

one serving of fruit (*see menu tips*)

two to three servings of vegetables (*see menu tips*)

Twice a week

one serving of either cooked liver or canned oysters (*see menu tips*)

Once a week

one cod liver oil softgel (130 IU). If your rat won't eat this plain, cut the softgel open and pour the oil over the molasses mix. (Do not give cod liver oil if your rat's calcium supplement contains vitamin D.)

RECIPE FOR MOLASSES MIX

THE MOLASSES MIX RECIPE LASTS ABOUT A week for two rats, depending on size. For more than two rats, multiply the recipe.

50 mcg vitamin B_{12}
40 mg manganese (capsules)
4 t shelled sunflower seeds
1 T flax seeds
¾ C Total cereal
3 T raw oatmeal
4 t pearled barley
4 t millet
3 T cooked brown rice
4 T cooked wheat germ
2¼ T nutritional yeast flakes (5.6 g)
1 lb package (not bulk) of soft tofu
1500 mg calcium (from chewable tablets or liquid calcium
    with vitamin D)
2000 mcg chromium picolinate
2 T blackstrap (dark or full flavor) molasses

Soak the calcium, chromium picolinate, and B_{12} tablets in a little water and crush. Coarsely crush the Total in a plastic bag. Mash the tofu in a bowl. Heat the molasses in the microwave for 5-15 seconds until warm. Add all the ingredients together with the warm molasses and mix thoroughly. Store covered in the refrigerator or freezer.

MENU TIPS

IT'S BEST TO USE A VARIETY OF COOKED DRY BEANS
to take advantage of their different nutrients. Frozen fruits and
veggies are almost as nutritious as fresh as long as they are used
before they get freezer burn. When feeding your rats grapes, feed
them purple grapes (instead of green grapes), which have cancer-
prevention compounds. You can thaw frozen foods in the
microwave, but be careful not to overcook! The beans, sweet
potato, broccoli, kale, and bok choy (if bok choy is not available,
substitute broccoli) are required. The other fruits and vegetables
can be substituted. Cook the beans and sweet potato—if your rat
doesn't like the other vegetables raw, cook them lightly. If you
are unable to buy Total cereal, you'll need to add a vitamin/
mineral supplement to the molasses mix. In that case, grind up a
chewable vitamin/mineral made for children two to four years
old and add to the molasses mix recipe; do not give the cod liver
oil capsule.

Serving Sizes (for a 1-pound rat)
cooked beans: 2 t
cooked sweet potato: ¾-inch cube
broccoli floret: 1½ inches across (cooked or raw)
leafy greens: 2-inch square piece
other veggies: 1-inch cube
bok choy: ¼ leaf
liver: 1 inch x ¼ inch x ¼ inch
canned oysters: 1 oyster
fruit: ½-inch cube
raisins: 3 to 4

SUGGESTED MENU

Monday	Tuesday	Wednesday	Thursday	Friday	Saturday	Sunday
berries	banana	grape/raisin	melon	apple	banana	plum/prune
kale	broccoli	beans	broccoli	kale	broccoli	bok choy
sprouts	tomato	bok choy	corn	squash	peas	carrot
beans	sweet potato	parsley	liver or oysters	beans	sweet potato	liver or oysters
	cod liver oil softgel					

Suggested Additional Treats

If your rats eat all the regular diet and still seem hungry, here are some treats you can offer them:

Any fruits

Any vegetables except those listed below

Mealworms (one to three daily)

Yogurt (1 t)

Carob chips (one daily)

Cooked spaghetti (it wiggles!)

Mushrooms

Never give your rats:

Carbonated beverages

Orange juice (males only)

Raw beans or peanuts

Raw sweet potato

Raw red cabbage and brussels sprouts

Raw artichokes

Raw bulk (non-packaged) tofu

Green bananas

Green potato skin and eyes

Chromium Picolinate

CHROMIUM PICOLINATE HAS BEEN SHOWN TO EXTEND THE average life span of rats. To find the dosage for your rat, multiply his weight in pounds by 189. For example, the dosage for a rat who weighs 0.75 pounds (12 oz.) is 142 micrograms (mcg).

If you have several rats of different weights, you might be able to give some of them the same dose. To figure the maximum dose (in mcg) your rat should get, multiply his weight in pounds by 227. You don't want to give a rat more than this, because too much chromium picolinate interferes with the absorption of other minerals. If you already feed your rat the molasses mix from the homemade rat diet, you do not need to give him any more chromium picolinate.

A good way to feed your rats chromium picolinate is to mix it in their favorite foods. Here are some recipes for tasty treats your rats are sure to love.

CREAM CHEESE BALLS

1 T Philadelphia FREE brand cream cheese spread

40-day dosage of chromium picolinate

1 t peanut butter (optional)

Mix together the cream cheese spread and chromium picolinate (add peanut butter for flavoring if desired). If too stiff, add more cheese. If too soft, add some flour. Form into a rectangle on wax paper and cut into forty small squares. Roll each into a ball and coat with flour. Freeze half and keep the remaining balls in the refrigerator. Give one ball to a rat each evening.

Note: Chromium picolinate is often pink and may make the balls pink—this is normal.

PEANUT BUTTER COOKIES
(recipe by Cindy Lee)

2 T whole wheat flour

1 t peanut butter

1–3 t fruit juice

40-day dosage of chromium picolinate

Mix the flour and chromium picolinate. Cut in the peanut butter with a knife. Add just enough juice to hold the dough together. Knead lightly and roll out on a floured plate. Cut into forty equal-sized pieces. Bake at 350° F for five to eight minutes (a toaster oven works great). Cookies should be slightly chewy. Store in an airtight container in the refrigerator. Feed one cookie to a rat each evening.

Appendix 2

RAT CLUBS

THESE ARE THE MAIN CLUBS IN THE UNITED STATES, Canada, and Great Britain. Contact each club to see if there is a chapter near you. (Information can change at any time.)

American Fancy Rat and Mouse Association
9230 64th Street
Riverside, CA 92509-5924
(909) 685-2350
Web site: www.afrma.org/afrma

Northern Illinois Rat Organization
Web site: www.niro-usa.org

Rat & Mouse Club of America
6082 Modoc Road
Westminster, CA 92683
Web site: www.rmca.org/

The Rat Fan Club
Debbie "The Rat Lady" Ducommun
857 Lindo Lane
Chico, CA 95973

  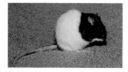

(530) 899-0605 (if your call does not go through, leave a message at 800-728-5052)
e-mail: ratlady@sunset.net
Web site: www.ratfanclub.org

(For more information on rat health care, consult her booklet, *Rat Health Care*, available from The Rat Fan Club. She is also willing to answer questions over the phone; please leave a message.)

National Fancy Rat Society
P.O. Box 24207
London, SE9 5ZF England
(011 44) 132-228-5788
Web site: www.nfrs.org

PUBLICATIONS

THE FOLLOWING PUBLICATIONS ARE OF SPECIAL note for their pictures and information.

Critters U.S.A.

An annual magazine covering all aspects of rat and small animal care, published by Fancy Publications

Pro-Rat-a

A bimonthly newsletter for members of the National Fancy Rat Society

Rat & Mouse Tales

A bimonthly magazine for members of AFRMA

Rat-tat Chat

An eight-page quarterly newsletter for members of the Rat Assistance & Teaching Society (RATS), a nonprofit organization working to educate pet-care professionals about pet rats.

857 Lindo Lane
Chico, CA 95973
(530) 899-0605
Web site: www.petrats.org

Glossary

agouti: a color of rat fur resulting from the banding of brown, black, and gray on the same strand of fur

albino: an organism lacking pigmentation of the fur, skin, and eyes. An albino rat has white fur and pink eyes.

bumblefoot (ulcerative pododermatitis): a bacterial infection affecting the feet of rats, commonly caused by pressure from wires of the rat cage

burrow: a tunnel complex in the ground made by wild rats for shelter and habitation. Many rats work together to build a burrow.

diastema: a space between the molars and incisor teeth. Rats have special cheek folds that fill in this space and prevent debris from entering the mouth when they are gnawing

domesticate: to shape a species of animal over time by selective breeding to live with and assist humans

estrus: a recurring period of time (usually every four to five days) when a female rat ovulates, is fertile, and is sexually receptive to males

guard hairs: the longest, thickest hairs in an animal's coat that provide the outer protective layer

heatstroke: a potentially fatal condition in rats caused by over-exposure to high temperatures

hemoglobin: a component of blood that contains iron and carries oxygen

hooded: a common color pattern in rats; white with color covering the head and shoulders and a stripe or patch of color down the back

hydration: the level of fluids in the body

incisors: the four front teeth, designed specifically for cutting. A rat's incisors grow continually throughout his or her life.

molar: a tooth with a rounded or flattened surface used for grinding. Rats have twelve tiny molars.

mycoplasmosis: a respiratory disease caused by the organism *Mycoplasma pulmonis*. It is incurable and contagious.

neuter: to surgically remove the testicles of a male animal and the uterus and ovaries of a female animal

Norway rat: *Rattus norvegicus*, also known as the brown or common rat, is the ancestor of the domestic rat. It has a heavy build suited to cool climates.

omnivorous: eating both plant and animal matter

paraplegia: paralysis of the legs and lower parts of the body

pattern: a genetically determined arrangement of color on a rat's body

pituitary gland: a small endocrine gland beneath the brain, often called the master gland because it controls many other glands

porphyrin: a brownish-red pigment present in a rat's tears

postpartum estrus: estrus that occurs within twenty-four hours of a female rat giving birth. For this reason, any fertile male rats should be removed from the cage before a birth.

rex: a genetic variety of rat in which the guard hairs are very short or missing and the hair and whiskers are curly or crinkled

roof rat: *Rattus rattus*, a small rat also known as the ship or tree rat, has a delicate build suited for tropical climates

socialization: the process during which an animal bonds to people or other animals through social interaction and handling. Early socialization with people makes it easier for a rat to bond to other people later on.

socialization period: phase of a rat's life, two to six weeks of age, when he or she most easily forms social bonds. For the rat to develop healthy relationships with humans or other animals, it is important for the rat to be held and petted during this time and to have social interaction with other rats.

spay: to surgically remove the ovaries and uterus of a female animal tame: to get an individual wild animal accustomed to the presence of humans

ticked: flecked hair banded with two or more colors

tumor: an abnormal growth in or on the body that is usually harmful and should be removed surgically if possible

Index

The photographs in this book are courtesy of: Jerry Boucher, cover, 20 (top), 23, 34 (top and bottom), 44, 64, 88, 98, 162, 163, 169, 170, 173; Amy Behrens, cover, 3, 132; Jennifer Dunlap, pp. 2, 28, 106, 120, 121; Patricia Hussey, pp. 5, 6, 36, 63, 73, 81, 84, 102, 104, 123 (bottom), 133, 137, 144, 145, 159, 180, 181; Rob Love, p.8; Bruce Ecker, pp. 9, 74 (top), 89; Leo Figiel, p. 10; Jim Klima, p. 11; Jerry P. Clark, p. 15 (top); Tom Myers, p. 15 (bottom); Debbie Ducommun, pp. 16, 25, 41, 47, 55, 56, 61, 66, 91, 95, 101, 107, 108, 110, 114, 115, 128, 138, 146, 174, 183; Klaus Schmidt, pp. 18, 83, 113, 135; Tarja Savinen, pp. 20 (bottom), 78, 142, 165 (top); Craig Robbins, pp. 24, 27, 152, 154, 156 (top), 165 (bottom); Dawn Kozak, pp. 29, 119, 130, 141, 151; Petra Tresbach, p. 30; Sherri Seymour, p. 39; Claude Seymour, pp. 45, 69; Nancy Hines, p. 48; Mary Ann Isaksen, pp. 50, 134; Diane Newburg, p. 52; Judith Lissenberg, p. 53; Catherine White, p. 70; Lisa Westplate, pp. 74 (bottom), 123 (top); Ruby Cook, p. 77; Lisa Hitchcock, p. 80; Sue Fanelli, p. 87; Johanna Mac Leod, p. 117; Larry Ducommun, pp. 125, 149; Ellie Mastropaolo, p. 150; Karla Barber, p. 156 (bottom); Larry Ferris, p. 161; Susan Sodergren, p. 179.